My Journey
& Relevant Quotes
TO EDIFY THE SOUL

Obinna D. Ezulike

OTMAD PUBLISHERS

MY JOURNEY & RELEVANT QUOTES
(TO EDIFY THE SOUL)

Cover Design: OTMAD

Printed by CreateSpace, an Amazon.com Company
1st Edition 2018

Acknowledgements

The title page benefits from the template created by Peter Wilson and modified by Velimir Gayevskiy (`https://www.latextemplates.com/template/vertical-line-title-page`). The modified template was last accessed in April 2018.

Many quotes might have been inaccessible to the author but for the electronic books freely shared by several individuals and organizations in the public domain. The Google digitization project has been of great help in this regard.

All scripture quotations are taken from the King James Version of the Bible available in the public domain.

Dedication

Thanks be to God Almighty for the gift of life and sanity of mind. As they say, "you never know what you've got until it's gone." I don't want to fall into that trap.

Appreciation goes to all who have positively influenced my life through discussions, books and audio-visual recordings. It is my honour to have had the blessed privilege of your time and resources.

This special thanks goes to my mother: Mrs. Ifeoma Christiana Ezulike. Her faithful dedication as a Christian, godly example and mother during twenty-five years of marriage has been impressive. She is the first human from whom I gleaned how one can harmonize profession with practice. My goal isn't to flatter her as many sons do. Instead, I'm grateful to God for her Christlike example before her children in those formative years.

Introduction

The 700+ quotes in this book were collected over 7+ years of personal study. You might then ask, "And so what?" Well, one unique feature of this book is that it isn't just another compilation of random quotes. These quotes were carefully distilled after a diligent study of 70+ books (not just from a book of quotes) and audio-visual recordings that have positively shaped my life. Therefore, I highly recommend these materials to interested readers. Their publication dates range from several centuries ago to contemporary times; and they cover a variety of topics like success, values, well-being, leadership, friendship, marriage and parenting. Many quotes are adapted from the collection available on my personal website (`http://sunset-to-sunrise.appspot.com/quotes.html`) as at March 2018. They are then applied in the form of short commentaries that are based on biblical principles.

The alphabetical arrangement of this book is based on author name (usually first name). Also, the alphabetical arrangement of quotes from each author is based on publication title (except when this format might hinder communication with the reader). The source of each quote is carefully documented as epigraphs. Also, the English dialect for each quote has been preserved as it is. An index list of 450+ topical entries is provided at the end to help readers navigate this book. For brevity and conciseness, the masculine is often used to represent humanity in general.

This book promises something for everyone. It could remind you of things once known but forgotten. It could point out things you know but haven't practised lately. It could shed new light on things you already practise. Also, it could open new topics for exploration. Please cover any faults or mistakes in this book with love and mercy. If you would kindly send a message across (`o.d.ezulike@googlemail.com`), I'd be willing to personally address them with you if so wished or (and) in subsequent editions of this book. God bless.

Contents

G

H

J

Index List

A

A. W. Pink
A. W. Tozer
Albert Einstein
Alexander, Archibald B. C.
Alexander Pope
Alexis de Tocqueville
Alfred Edersheim
Anonymous
Arnold Dallimore

A. W. Pink

... the present decay of home life and family discipline
threaten the stability of our nation today
far more severely than does any foreign hostility

The Excellence of Marriage
A. W. PINK

Will Durant said, "No great nation is ever conquered until it has destroyed itself." Isn't the present decay in home life and family discipline evidence of this internal destruction? Some argue that home life and family discipline are "traditional" and "outdated" concepts; and as such, incompatible with our "modernity." Well, my humble submission is that societal decay will not cower in the face of a sly excuse. Let's call a spade, a spade. All this name-branding isn't helping matters. Even if I should agree that home life and family discipline are "old fashioned," it should be wise of me to practice them if they will improve my family and society.

A. W. Tozer

Neglected Christian truths
can be revitalized only when by prayer and long meditation
we isolate them from the mass of hazy ideas with which our minds are filled
and hold them steadily and determinedly in the focus of the mind's attention

God's Pursuit of Man, Chapter 1, p. 2
A. W. TOZER

This sort of long meditation can't be easily done in group or public. Although we shouldn't jettison public prayer, every Christian needs to effectively sharpen himself in private. Hence, the need for a personal and devotional walk with God. This is imperative since Christ's mission for His Bride, the Church, includes mutual exhortation and edification.

Nothing of God dies when a man of God dies

God's Pursuit of Man, Chapter 1, p. 4
A. W. TOZER

None is that indispensable before God. Do you think that God who is already at the end from the beginning will have a failed project?

The truest and most acceptable repentance
is to reverse the acts and attitudes of which we repent
A thousand years of remorse over a wrong act
would not please God as much as a change of conduct and a reformed life

God's Pursuit of Man, Chapter 5, p. 72
A. W. TOZER

This is still relevant today, when we have much false repentance with little evidence of rebirth. A man may fool everyone, including himself; but none can fool God.

Albert Einstein

If you believe that something is impossible
do not disturb the person who is doing it

ALBERT EINSTEIN

You only achieve what you believe. So, don't obstruct those working towards things you currently believe are impossible. However, differentiating between good and evil ends is another discussion.

Alexander, Archibald B. C.

Where there is no freedom of choice
we cannot speak of an action as either good or evil

Christianity and Ethics: A Handbook of Christian Ethics
Section A, Chapter I, p. 13
ALEXANDER, ARCHIBALD B. C.

This cuts to the heart of the nature of truth. If men are free to choose and truth isn't absolute, how should they differentiate right from wrong and good from evil? These terms simply become meaningless.

Our actions are, indeed, good when we do our duty because we ought
but they are beautiful when we do it because we cannot do otherwise
because they have become our second nature

Christianity and Ethics: A Handbook of Christian Ethics
Section A, Chapter I, p. 16
ALEXANDER, ARCHIBALD B. C.

O! Christian, do you delight in living according to God's Word? Above else, are you addicted to seeking and doing His Will for your life?

In Christ were gathered up
the wisdom of the Greek
the courage of the Roman
the righteousness of the Jew
and He who came not to destroy but to fulfil
at once interpreted and satisfied the longings of the ages

Christianity and Ethics: A Handbook of Christian Ethics
Section A, Chapter III, p. 52
ALEXANDER, ARCHIBALD B. C.

Jesus Christ is the true embodiment of all virtue. Apostle Paul described himself in 2 Corinthians 6:10, ". . . as having nothing, and yet possessing all things:" nothing according to worldly standards; but all things, since he is already hidden in Christ.

Worship is not a meaningless ebullition of feeling or a superstitious ritual
but a form of self-expression
which is to be enlightened and guided by thought

Christianity and Ethics: A Handbook of Christian Ethics
Section B, Chapter IV, p. 66
ALEXANDER, ARCHIBALD B. C.

This element of "thought" appears to be one missing link in much of today's worship. No wonder many younger folks can't connect to hymns. Worship isn't purely emotional; it has a meditative component as well.

Life is a great and solemn trust committed to each by God
for the use or abuse of which every man will be called to account

---

Christianity and Ethics: A Handbook of Christian Ethics
Section B, Chapter VI, p. 94
ALEXANDER, ARCHIBALD B. C.

This places self-murder, assisted self-murder and outright murder in a clearer perspective. Life isn't meant to be disposed of at anyone's whim.

Christianity does not destroy 'the will to live,'
but only the will to live at all costs

Christianity and Ethics: A Handbook of Christian Ethics
Section C, Chapter VIII, p. 128
ALEXANDER, ARCHIBALD B. C.

This shows the proper place of self-preservation in Jesus Christ; just as He taught in Matthew 16:24-26, Mark 8:34-38 and Luke 9:23-26 respectively.

Life cannot be always a compromise
Sooner or later it must become an alternative

Christianity and Ethics: A Handbook of Christian Ethics
Section C, Chapter X, p. 174
Alexander, Archibald B. C.

A paraphrase of one of Vance Havner's quotes which talks about those "who live a life that's neither-nor in a world that's either-or" is apt here. Although compromise has its place in life, it still ought to be circumscribed by righteous convictions.

Alexander Pope

The sprightly Sylvia trips along the green
She runs, but hopes she does not run unseen
While a kind glance at her pursuer flies
How much at variance are her feet and eyes!

Spring: The First Pastorals, Lines 57-60
ALEXANDER POPE, THE MAJOR WORKS

This is a beautiful painting of the complexity involved in human communication.

Words are like leaves; and where they most abound
Much fruit of sense beneath is rarely found

Essay on Criticism, Lines 309-310
ALEXANDER POPE, THE MAJOR WORKS

Be silent always when you doubt your sense;
And speak, though sure, with seeming diffidence

Essay on Criticism, Lines 566-567
ALEXANDER POPE, THE MAJOR WORKS

As they say, "Silence can be golden." Talkativeness is a broom which sweeps meaningfulness out. It is a symptom of an underlying issue; a symptom that can glow so bright as to fool people into thinking all is well.

True ease in writing comes from art, not chance
As those move easiest who have learned to dance

Essay on Criticism, Lines 362-363
ALEXANDER POPE, THE MAJOR WORKS

As they say, "Practice makes perfect." The same applies to effective expression and communication in writing. What are you waiting for? Start today.

For fools rush in where angels fear to tread

Essay on Criticism, Lines 625
Alexander Pope, The Major Works

If zeal isn't tempered with appropriate wisdom, trouble might not be far away. Don't overestimate your strengths or underestimate your weaknesses.

Vice is a monster of so frightful mien
As, to be hated, needs to be seen
Yet seen too oft, familiar with her face
We first endure, then pity, then embrace

An Essay on Man, Epistle II, Lines 217-220
Alexander Pope, The Major Works

Note the sequence: endure, pity and embrace. Matthew Henry said that, "Familiarity, even with that which is most awful, is apt to breed contempt." Repeated exposure to a thing increases a man's sympathy towards it; and at last, might make him a zealous convert. Vance Havner used to say that "The worst of all is that such people get so used to the dark that they think it is growing brighter. Sit long enough in a dark room and you will imagine that more light is breaking in. Men who dwell too long in darkness fancy the day is dawning. ... One may live in a twilight zone, in conditions of low visibility, until he finds the practices of this world less repulsive. He mistakes the stretching of his conscience for the broadening of his mind."

Alexis de Tocqueville

Liberty... considers religion as the guardian of morality
morality as the guarantee of law and the security that freedom will last

Democracy in America, p. 56
ALEXIS DE TOCQUEVILLE

Notice how liberty, religion, morality, law and freedom form a tight chain. If one link is broken, the rest soon falls apart. Today, a badly-defined "freedom" is replacing true liberty, demonizing religion and declaring morality as relative. Isn't it scary seeing the pack of cards gradually crumble while we're busy stacking more cards on top?

Where family feeling ends
self-centeredness directs a man's true inclinations

Democracy in America, p. 63
ALEXIS DE TOCQUEVILLE

According to William Gairdner, there has truly been a "war on the family" over the years. The only new thing is its darker dimension. Is it any wonder that we have bred and still breed much narcissistic egomaniacs?

Variations in intellect come directly from God
and men cannot prevent this being so...
although the intelligence of men is different...
there is at its disposal an equal means of development

Democracy in America, p. 63
ALEXIS DE TOCQUEVILLE

Equality of outcome is a practical impossibility; except in a world of automata. Equality of opportunity is a possible practicality; which is just and desirable. The next time someone starts speaking of creating an "equal" society, ask him to define his meaning of equality.

Throughout time, it has been observed that familiarity with the law
was a poor training for a man's exercise of administrative authority
...the policing of society is a task
which demands good sense and integrity more than legal knowledge

Democracy in America, p. 88-89
Alexis de Tocqueville

Jeff Allen the Comedian once said, "...that's the America I grew up in...before the lawyers took it over and ruined it..." Although funny, it's a good commentary on this quote. How many political leaders who are lawyers by training have good sense and integrity? Ben Carson once said in a national speech and I paraphrase, "...lawyers are taught to win, by hook or crook..." On the other hand, how many spiritual leaders who are graduates of theological seminaries have good sense and integrity?

...Natural weakness of democracies
is the gradual subordination of all the state powers
to the slightest wishes of the majority...

Democracy in America, p. 159
Alexis de Tocqueville

The all-desirable "democracy" has side-effects which must be wisely counterbalanced to ensure a stable and sustainable society. For one, democracy has a way of breeding sycophants as leaders; those "experts in doubletalk and the art of almost saying something" as Vance Havner once put it.

In general, only simple ideas take hold of the minds of a people
A false yet clear and precise idea
will always have more potency in society at large
than a true but complex one

Democracy in America, p. 193
Alexis de Tocqueville

This shows how the majority is prone to being swindled by "smooth operators." It also emphasizes the convincing power found in clarity and

precision of expression. Learn to express truth in simple and clear terms
as possible.

...that sort of everyday practical wisdom
and that knowledge of the small business of life which we call common sense

---

Democracy in America, p. 267
ALEXIS DE TOCQUEVILLE

This is one succinct way to define common sense.

...Democratic laws
generally tend toward the good of the greatest possible number
for they stem from the majority of all the citizens
a majority which may be in error
but which could not follow a path contrary to its own interests

---

Democracy in America, p. 270
ALEXIS DE TOCQUEVILLE

...the real advantage of democratic government
is not to guarantee the interests of all as has sometimes been the claim
but simply to protect those of the greatest

Democracy in America, p. 281
ALEXIS DE TOCQUEVILLE

It is unfortunate that many today, including political leaders, get this
concept of democracy twisted.

Omnipotence seems self-evidently a bad and dangerous thing
Its exercise appears to be beyond man's powers, whoever he might be
and I see that only God can be omnipotent without danger
because his wisdom and justice are always equal to his power
There is therefore no earthly authority
so worthy of respect or vested with so sacred a right
that I would wish to allow it unlimited action and unrestricted dominance

---

Democracy in America, p. 294
ALEXIS DE TOCQUEVILLE

Power that isn't circumscribed by wisdom and justice quickly turns into tyranny. The greater the power, the greater the wisdom and justice required to keep it in check. A man who answers to none apart from himself is already a tyrant or about to manifest as one.

In Europe
almost all social disorder stems from disturbances at home
and not far removed from the marriage bed

Democracy in America, p. 341
Alexis de Tocqueville

This has worldwide application today. Is it any wonder that the increase in suicides, murders, teenage pregnancies, abortions and mental disorders correlates with the increase in divorces and marital perversions?

Alfred Edersheim

... as was rightly said
mistakes impressed upon the young mind
were afterwards not easily corrected

Sketches of Jewish Social Life in the Days of Christ
Chapter VIII, p. 130
ALFRED EDERSHEIM

As such, parents should prayerfully and carefully watch over their young wards. Many schools today are no more places of education and enlightenment; but mental institutions of indoctrination, manned by "mind benders," as Tim Lahaye once put it.

Education begins in the home...
it is imparted by influence and example before it comes by teaching
it is acquired by what is seen and heard
before it is laboriously learned from books
its real object becomes instinctively felt before its goal is consciously sought

---

The Life and Times of Jesus The Messiah
Vol. I, Book II, Chapter IX, p. 227
ALFRED EDERSHEIM

What a fine commentary on Proverbs 22:6. Parents stand the best chance of positively impacting their children. Don't forfeit or exchange this blessed privilege for any thing.

Anonymous

People with narrow minds usually have broad tongues

ANONYMOUS

Talkativeness has never been a virtue. It is one sure way of releasing airy weightlessness from the vast emptiness of a mind.

There are only two lasting bequests we can give our children
one is roots, the other wings

ANONYMOUS

This is an important message for parents and mentors. They ought to root their wards in values such as truth, honesty and justice. Also, they should encourage and support them to realize their God-given potentials.

Arnold Dallimore

God give me a deep humility, a well-guided zeal, a burning love
and a single eye, and then let men or devils do their worst!

The Life and Times of The Great Evangelist of the 18th Century Revival
Vol. 1, p. 140
GEORGE WHITEFIELD
IN ARNOLD DALLIMORE

Ensure that you are not part of your problem. All the sources of our challenges aren't external.

...we can preach the Gospel no further
than we have experienced the Power of it in our own hearts

The Life and Times of The Great Evangelist of the 18th Century Revival
Vol. 1, p. 434
GEORGE WHITEFIELD
IN ARNOLD DALLIMORE

Although preaching is great, "we can't give what we don't have."

Be humble, talk little, think and pray much

The Life and Times of The Great Evangelist of the 18th Century Revival
Vol. 1, p. 577
GEORGE WHITEFIELD
IN ARNOLD DALLIMORE

This is much needed today when feeling, talkativeness and showman-
ship have been elevated above thinking, quietness and modesty.

I have no thoughts of settling till I settle in glory

The Life and Times of The Great Evangelist of the 18th Century Revival
Vol. 2, p. 220
GEORGE WHITEFIELD
IN ARNOLD DALLIMORE

There is no retirement for Christians here on earth. Any who does otherwise will definitely be left behind. As the songwriter penned, "Keep on the firing line." Vance Havner once said and I paraphrase, "...if you feather your nest too well, you won't [be able to] fly..."

...I would only caution thee against taking anything for Gospel
upon the mere authority of man

The Life and Times of The Great Evangelist of the 18th Century Revival
Vol. 2, p. 233
GEORGE WHITEFIELD
IN ARNOLD DALLIMORE

Carefully weigh every opinion, teaching or preaching against Scriptures. No man is above mistake or error: intentionally or unintentionally.

Go where thou wilt
though thou shouldest be in the purest society under heaven
thou wilt find that the best of men are but men at the best...

The Life and Times of The Great Evangelist of the 18th Century Revival
Vol. 2, p. 233
GEORGE WHITEFIELD
IN ARNOLD DALLIMORE

Biblical perfection on earth doesn't mean angelic perfection. However, this is no license or cloak for sin and wickedness. God's Grace is sufficient to help us live above our temperamental quirks and idiosyncrasies.

...the best preparation for preaching on Sundays
is to preach everyday in the week

The Life and Times of The Great Evangelist of the 18th Century Revival
Vol. 2, p. 286
GEORGE WHITEFIELD
IN ARNOLD DALLIMORE

This message isn't only for preachers in the pulpit. It is for every Christian. Christianity is meant to be an everyday lifestyle.

I find a love of power sometimes intoxicates even God's own dear children
and makes them to mistake passion for zeal
and an overbearing spirit for an authority given them from above

The Life and Times of The Great Evangelist of the 18th Century Revival
Vol. 2, p. 339
GEORGE WHITEFIELD
IN ARNOLD DALLIMORE

Error has a sly way of creeping into a man's life. It doesn't mind entering through the gate disguised as truth or boldly jumping over the fence undetected. This calls for daily examination of our motives under the Light of Scriptures.

When the spirit of prayer began to be lost, the forms of prayer were invented

The Life and Times of The Great Evangelist of the 18th Century Revival
Vol. 2, p. 470
GEORGE WHITEFIELD IN TYERMAN'S WHITEFIELD, VOL. 2, P. 545
IN ARNOLD DALLIMORE

Structure and guidelines have their proper places in life. However, their wrong use can stifle or even replace genuineness.

B

B. K. Eakman
Ben Carson & Gregg Lewis
Bertrand Russell
Bill Newman
Blaine Bartel
Blaise Pascal
Brian Tracy
Bruce Barton

B. K. Eakman

The epitaph of the 20th Century should be:
"Here lie the victims of open-mindedness"

Cloning of the American Mind, Introduction, p. 21
JOSEPH SOBRAN
IN B. K. EAKMAN

Open-mindedness isn't evil. Like most things however, it turns into a monster when taken to the extreme. It can make someone a prime target for conmen and tricksters.

Insights... by those whom we would call ancient peoples
remind us how unschooled most of us are in this modern era

Cloning of the American Mind, Chapter 23, p. 421
B. K. EAKMAN

Being better informed doesn't necessarily mean better schooled. Without doing much harm to the quote, true education could be substituted for schooling here. True education is that which places facts before a man and equips him with relevant tools for making a reasonable choice. Someone might end up parroting meaningless words if he can't make balanced sense of the much information in his possession.

Many viewers —
particularly those without firmly entrenched beliefs of their own
will soak up the hidden political agenda and attitudinal messages
without thinking about it; they will internalize the messages.
Why? Because most TV shows don't challenge thought on a rational level;
TV generally functions on the emotional and subliminal levels

---

Cloning of the American Mind, Chapter 24, p. 466
B. K. EAKMAN

This message is still relevant today. Whoever accuses you of "indoctrinating" your ward with "old fashioned" beliefs is an hypocrite: be it government, organisation or individual. This is because whatever solution they propose is still an indoctrination. Ravi Zacharias once said, "How do you reach a generation that listens with its eyes and thinks with its feelings?" He also mentions, "the front door of reason" and "the back door of the imagination." We ought to carefully guard that "back door."

Ben Carson & Gregg Lewis

If you were to destroy in man the belief of immortality
not only love, but every living force maintaining the life of the world
would at once be dried up...
if God does not exist, everything is permitted

Take The Risk
FYODOR DOSTOEVSKY
IN BEN CARSON & GREGG LEWIS

This is not to bash anyone's faith. However, if morality is purely a social construct or relative at best, how should we differentiate good from evil? Moral relativity denies the existence of God. If God doesn't exist, society will totter towards nihilism, fatalism, and eventual collapse.

Bertrand Russell

The whole problem with the world is that
fools and fanatics are always so certain of themselves
and wiser people so full of doubts

BERTRAND RUSSELL

A man's confidence is no conclusive proof of the rightness of his action. If you believe your goal is right, then evaluate the sincerity and wisdom of your motives. Once this is clarified, act decisively and courageously despite the oppositions you might face.

Bill Newman

Persist and persevere. Overnight success is a myth

Soaring With Eagles, Principles Of Success
BILL NEWMAN

True success without work doesn't exist. Success without work might appear praiseworthy at first, but it usually ends in shame and destruction.

Worry is like a rocking chair
it will give you something to do but it won't get you anywhere

---

Soaring With Eagles, Principles Of Success
BILL NEWMAN

This is a quite a hard one to swallow. It is easier read and said than done. Worry is an unproductive occupation. As they say, "Activity doesn't necessarily translate to productivity."

The greatest tragedy to befall a person is: to have sight but lack vision

---

Soaring With Eagles, Principles Of Success
HELLEN KELLER IN BILL NEWMAN

The physical eyes can only carry a man so far. However, the eyes of the mind is far more important.

Blaine Bartel

Preparation time is never wasted time

Reality Check
BLAINE BARTEL

Never write preparation off just because its results aren't often imme-diate. After all, opportunity never announces its arrival beforehand.

Blaise Pascal

Our achievements today are but the sum of our thoughts of yesterday

BLAISE PASCAL

Thoughts are cumulative. They are like muscle fibres which determine the strength of our achievements. Be deliberate in what you feed your mind. It can be such an uphill task to later nullify the effects of wrong thoughts.

The heart has its reasons which reason knows not of

BLAISE PASCAL

Reason is a wonderful vehicle for clarifying thoughts but a limited organ for deepest understanding. One good example is love. Love moves a man to give to another without foreseeing any sign of returns in the nearest future.

Brian Tracy

If your opportunity comes and you are not prepared for it
it will only make you look foolish

Create Your Own Future
EARL NIGHTINGALE
IN BRIAN TRACY

The right time for preparation is before opportunity arrives; because it rarely gives advance notice. Do you have a vision for your life? What preparations are you making today to get there?

On the beaches of hesitation lie the bleached bones of millions
who at the moments of victory, rested and in resting, lost all

Create Your Own Future
FAMOUS QUOTE
IN BRIAN TRACY

Patience, persistence and perseverance will help a man reap the effort and time already invested towards his goal(s). These 3 P's can make all the difference. How patient, persistent and persevering are you? Do you give up at the first sign of opposition?

If your real desire is to do good
there is no need to wait for money before you do it
You can do it now, at this very moment, and just where you are

Create Your Own Future
JAMES ALLEN
IN BRIAN TRACY

There is deep truth embedded in the popular saying that, "The best things in life are free." Think of it: sacrificial givers are the ones who have made the most positive impact on your life. They owed you no obligation and yet willingly gave their time and resources. Some of them had or have little of this world's riches. Yet, they invested their prayer, time and counsel in your life. Money is good but isn't the ultimate. I hope this will spur you into action today.

Honesty is the first chapter in the book of wisdom

Create Your Own Future
THOMAS JEFFERSON
IN BRIAN TRACY

The prevalent decadence seems to say otherwise. Society is prone to extol men who achieve external success without questioning how they got there. These men are lauded as smart, innovative and progressive. However, true success is tied to wisdom. Wisdom is the preserver of success: preventing a man from dabbling into dubious means in the first place. This points to the pivotal relationship of honesty with wisdom. Honesty will constrain a man to side with the right, even if it will cost him much. How honest are you?

You miss every shot you don't take

Create Your Own Future
WAYNE GRETZKY
IN BRIAN TRACY

Don't be afraid to take a chance: to try something different. It is better to try and fail than accept failure without putting up a fight. However, ensure that this "shot" is a virtuous one.

The depth of the foundation
determines how high the structure can be erected

Create Your Own Future
BRIAN TRACY

Don't get carried away with the pace at which many are building their "skyscrapers" today. Often, the slowest path is the surest. Ensure that your foundation is on tested grounds: grounds such as truth, honesty, integrity, justice and equity.

Every extraordinary achievement is the result of
thousands of ordinary achievements that no one ever sees or appreciates

Create Your Own Future
BRIAN TRACY

Greatness doesn't happen all of a sudden. It is an accumulation of little "great things." Keep working at it.

You can't hit a target that you can't see

Create Your Own Future
BRIAN TRACY

Now is the time to start or improve the training of your mind's eye. A mission without a vision is destined for frustration.

. . . a person of average intelligence with clear goals
will run circles around a genius who is not sure what he or she really wants

Goals!, p. x
BRIAN TRACY

As John Maxwell says, "Talent is never enough." Talent is important but isn't the ultimate. It must be mixed with the right ingredients (focus, passion, hope, dedication and the rest) to amount to anything worthwhile.

The elevator to success is out of service. But the stairs are always open

Goals!, p. 15
ZIG ZIGLAR
IN BRIAN TRACY

There are no short-cuts to success. Although levers might be available, you still need to do the work of pulling them.

Life is lived from the inside out

Goals!, p. 40
ZIG ZIGLAR
IN BRIAN TRACY

The heart is the right starting point. Is your heart right with God? As Vance Havner once said and I paraphrase, "...what good is it mopping the floor while the faucet is running?" Change your heart, change your life.

The "Winning Edge" concept says:
Small differences can lead to enormous differences in results

---

The 100 Absolutely Unbreakable Laws of Business Success
BRIAN TRACY

Little things multiply into big things when consistently done over time. The life transformation you desire might just require doing things differently, one little thing at a time.

Elephants don't bite; rather it is the mosquitoes

The 100 Absolutely Unbreakable Laws of Business Success
BRIAN TRACY

Big issues often obstruct our paths in ways that drive us to address them quickly. However, it is those small issues which we neglect or don't detect that eventually causes so much discomfort.

The bitterness of poor quality is remembered long after
the pleasure of low price has been forgotten

The 100 Absolutely Unbreakable Laws of Business Success
BRIAN TRACY

If you will deliver services at low price(s), do so at reasonable quality. Else, many customers will gladly pay extra for better quality elsewhere. Low price alone isn't necessarily a good selling-point or business strategy.

You must deal with life as it is, not as you wish it were or could be

---

The 100 Absolutely Unbreakable Laws of Business Success
BRIAN TRACY

Every man has to start at his present condition. This is the only option: deal with it. Start working on it and stop wishing it away.

It's not how much you make
but how much you keep that determines your financial future

The 100 Absolutely Unbreakable Laws of Business Success
BRIAN TRACY

This is equivalent to storing sand in a basket. You normally end up with next to nothing despite much effort and sand volume. Do you have financial goals and plans? How much do you set aside for investment? You know, helping the less privileged is a form of investment.

You can't fly with the eagles if you continue to scratch with the turkeys

The 100 Absolutely Unbreakable Laws of Business Success
BRIAN TRACY

Now is a good time to evaluate your companions. Are they heading in your intended direction? If necessary, today is the best day to change your close associates.

The very worst use of your time
is to do very well what need not be done at all

The 100 Absolutely Unbreakable Laws of Business Success
BRIAN TRACY

Be very selective how you spend your time. Don't dedicate your scarce resources to worthless goals. Remember that time lost can't be recovered.

You will always be paid in direct proportion to:
what you do, how well you do it, and the difficulty of replacing you

The 100 Absolutely Unbreakable Laws of Business Success
BRIAN TRACY

Ensure that you're "indispensable." Of course, no man is truly indispensable in the plain sense. However, you can give yourself this "indispensable" edge by learning new skills and honing existing ones. Be the very best at what you do. This requires a wise combination of raw talent and good doses of hard work.

Go the extra mile. There are never any traffic jams on the extra mile

The 100 Absolutely Unbreakable Laws of Business Success
BRIAN TRACY

Little competition exists in that zone of "extra." Vance Havner used to say that, "...the difference is worth the distance."

Desire, Decision, Discipline and Determination
can take you anywhere you want

The 100 Absolutely Unbreakable Laws of Business Success
BRIAN TRACY

Raw talent without a combination of these 4 D's can only take you so far. Don't allow your talent blind you to this truth.

Action orientation
is the most outwardly identifiable quality of a winning human being

The 100 Absolutely Unbreakable Laws of Business Success
BRIAN TRACY

Procrastination takes none far. Develop a healthy sense of urgency for the important things in life. Prioritize and act on them today.

The more you "try", the more you will "triumph"

The 100 Absolutely Unbreakable Laws of Business Success
BRIAN TRACY

The path to triumph is through the valley of "try." You lose nothing by trying. Even if you fail a couple of times, you learn how to avoid failing the same way in subsequent trials.

You can tell a big person by the way he treats little people

The 100 Absolutely Unbreakable Laws of Business Success
THOMAS CARLYLE
IN BRIAN TRACY

Great people are marked by humility and consideration of others, irrespective of status or belief. They put you at ease within few moments of meeting them.

Bruce Barton

Sometimes
when I consider what tremendous consequences come from little things...
I am tempted to think...there are no little things

BRUCE BARTON

Truth be told, there are little things in life. However, ensure that those "little" things are given appropriate attention. Else, it might be too late to realize that they are the keys to the "big" things.

C

C. S. Lewis
Catherine Marshall
Charles Spurgeon
Chinese Saying
Christian G. Weiss
Craig Groeschel

C. S. Lewis

You cannot make men good by law
and without good men you cannot have a good society

Mere Christianity, Book Three, Chapter 1, p. 68
THE COMPLETE C. S. LEWIS SIGNATURE CLASSICS

Quite a way to put it! Those who believe in the human perfectibility through societal reform and education need to weigh their convictions against history. So how can we make men good? Jesus Christ is the viable solution I have tested, proved and recommend.

If you are thinking of becoming a Christian, I warn you
you are embarking on something which is going to take the whole of you...
one of the reasons why it needs no special education to be a Christian is that
Christianity is an education itself

Mere Christianity, Book Three, Chapter 2, p. 71
THE COMPLETE C. S. LEWIS SIGNATURE CLASSICS

Is it any wonder we have a lot of half-baked, shallow-rooted and feel-good followers of Christ today? Many preachers peddle a false gospel which is not Christ's; which has no cost or cross. Their messages tickle people's "deaf" ears to worldliness rather than tingle them to the hearing of faith. They burnish their "cold" hearts to deadness rather than burn them to repentance unto good works. Have you really counted the cost since you became a Christian?

Every one says forgiveness is a lovely idea
until they have something to forgive...

Mere Christianity, Book Three, Chapter 7, p. 98
THE COMPLETE C. S. LEWIS SIGNATURE CLASSICS

Isn't this true about most of us? I'm not exempted. As they say, "The taste of the pudding is in the eating." What good is your profession if you haven't or can't put it into practice?

But love, in the Christian sense, does not mean an emotion
It is a state not of feelings but the will
the state of the will which we naturally have about ourselves
and must learn to have about other people

Mere Christianity, Book Three, Chapter 9, p. 109
THE COMPLETE C. S. LEWIS SIGNATURE CLASSICS

Christian Love, either towards God or towards man, is an affair of the will

Mere Christianity, Book Three, Chapter 9, p. 111
THE COMPLETE C. S. LEWIS SIGNATURE CLASSICS

No wonder marriage has become an endangered "specie." True friendship hasn't been spared either from this onslaught of emotionalism. Selfishness, disguised as love, has become the rule for many relationships. Help address this issue today by cross-checking your understanding and practice of love.

If you read history
you will find that the Christians who did most for the present world
were just those who thought most of the next

Mere Christianity, Book Three, Chapter 10, p. 112
THE COMPLETE C. S. LEWIS SIGNATURE CLASSICS

Aim at Heaven and you will get earth 'thrown in'
aim at earth and you will get neither

Mere Christianity, Book Three, Chapter 10, p. 112
THE COMPLETE C. S. LEWIS SIGNATURE CLASSICS

What a timely warning! However, you mustn't become so "other-worldly" minded as to be earthly useless. That would defeat the purpose, wouldn't it? We ought to fix our eyes on the right things and get our priorities straight. The rest will fall in line.

... 'feeling better' is not much good
if the thermometer shows that your temperature is still going up

---

Mere Christianity, Book Four, Chapter 10, p. 164
THE COMPLETE C. S. LEWIS SIGNATURE CLASSICS

We aren't natural lovers of truth. A great deal of humility is required to swallow one's pride and digest truth. In many circles today, any act which goes against someone's feelings is deemed rude and insensitive; regardless of its appropriateness. We easily forget that feelings are subjective, unstable and poor tools for evaluating truth.

There are people (a great many of them)
who are slowly ceasing to be Christians
but who still call themselves by that name: some of them are clergymen

---

Mere Christianity, Book Four, Chapter 10, p. 165
THE COMPLETE C. S. LEWIS SIGNATURE CLASSICS

This calls for watchfulness. Don't believe a man on the sole basis of his profession: verbally or vocationally. Weigh the consistency of his profession against his practice. Hypocrisy is a natural propensity common to all men. Therefore, why not start by examining yourself today?

Indeed, the safest road to Hell is the gradual one
— the gentle slope, soft underfoot
without sudden turnings, without milestones, without signposts

---

The Screwtape Letters, Chapter 12, p. 220
THE COMPLETE C. S. LEWIS SIGNATURE CLASSICS

Daily examine your life under the Light of Scriptures. No man in above falling into this trap of subtle descent.

The earliest converts
were converted by a single historical fact (the Resurrection)
and a single theological doctrine (the Redemption)
operating on a sense of sin which they already had

The Screwtape Letters, Chapter 23, p. 252
THE COMPLETE C. S. LEWIS SIGNATURE CLASSICS

This is a neat way of placing the theology of Salvation from sin in a sort of historical context.

The basic principle of the new education is to be that dunces and idlers
must not be made to feel inferior to intelligent and industrious pupils
That would be 'undemocratic'

Screwtape Proposes a Toast, p. 293
The Complete C. S. Lewis Signature Classics

Notice the twist and abuse of the word "democratic" here. In theory, does democracy guarantee or at least promote equality of outcome or equality of opportunity? Recently, there are moves in several educational groups to eliminate grades, promote every student irrespective of present performance and admit every applicant irrespective of past performance. Quite a messy pot of "malignant stew," as Vance Havner used to say.

The fine flower of unholiness can grow
only in the close neighborhood of the Holy

Screwtape Proposes a Toast, p. 296
The Complete C. S. Lewis Signature Classics

Where else can unholiness best disguise itself than under the radiant beauty of holiness? This allows it to exude a transient fluorescence that quickly fades once proximity with holiness is lost. A Christian ought to test everyone for the fruits of holiness; regardless of anyone's brilliant profession of faith.

...for the slaves of the senses
after the first bait, are starved by their masters

Miracles, Chapter 15, p. 415
The Complete C. S. Lewis Signature Classics

Sensual pleasure is one of God's gifts to man. However, it can quickly become a vice when taken beyond the bounds of virtue. Don't be deceived by the allure and promise of pleasure's bait(s). The last satisfaction a man gets will be the first one offered at the point of enslavement.

All prayers are heard, though not all prayers are granted

Miracles, Appendix B, p. 462
THE COMPLETE C. S. LEWIS SIGNATURE CLASSICS

Generally, God's response to prayer could be fulfilment (swift, delayed, forced) or denial: according to His Omnipotence and Omniscience. Someone said that "if God granted every prayer, many would be dead or living in regret."

There have been some who were so occupied in spreading Christianity
[that] they never gave a thought to Christ

The Great Divorce, Chapter 9, p. 505
THE COMPLETE C. S. LEWIS SIGNATURE CLASSICS

As Vance Havner said, and I paraphrase, "...someone can backslide into hell with a Bible as big as a Chicago directory under his arm...we can lose Christ in the midst of the work." This is a call for personal examination under the Light of Scriptures.

The sane would do no good if they made themselves mad to help madmen

---

The Great Divorce, Chapter 9, p. 506
THE COMPLETE C. S. LEWIS SIGNATURE CLASSICS

Many Christians have broken lose from the yoke of Christ in the process of becoming "like" unbelievers to win them to Christ. Every method of preaching and evangelism isn't safe for everyone. Some methods require a tenuous balance of wisdom, grace and discernment which a person may presently lack.

God whispers to us in our pleasures, speaks in our conscience
but shouts in our pain: it is His megaphone to rouse a deaf world

---

The Problem of Pain, Chapter 6, p. 604
THE COMPLETE C. S. LEWIS SIGNATURE CLASSICS

...Pain plants the flag of truth within a rebel fortress

The Problem of Pain, Chapter 8, p. 622
THE COMPLETE C. S. LEWIS SIGNATURE CLASSICS

What a succinct way to put it! As Elect Boogbaa would say, "...this gives me chills." Aren't we all deaf in various degrees to God's whispers? Pleasure has a way of blunting spiritual sensitivity. Although pleasure isn't evil, we have a proclivity of making it our master; and what a brutish master it is. Pain on the other hand often slows us down; long enough to take the spotlight away from ourselves. Pain has its advantages after all.

For a good wife contains so many persons in herself
...daughter...mother...pupil...teacher...subject...sovereign...
trusty comrade, friend, shipmate, fellow-soldier

A Grief Observed, Chapter Three, p. 676
The Complete C. S. Lewis Signature Classics

This is quite an extensive list. By extension, a similar one could be made for a good husband. Are you a good husband to your wife? Are you a good wife to your husband?

There is, hidden or flaunted, a sword between the sexes
till an entire marriage reconciles them

A Grief Observed, Chapter Three, p. 677
The Complete C. S. Lewis Signature Classics

A forewarning to the unmarried who desire marriage. Also, an encouragement to the married to prayerfully work it out.

And all the time — such is the tragic-comedy of our situation
— we continue to clamour for those very qualities we are rendering impossible
...In a sort of ghastly simplicity
we remove the organ and demand the function
We make men without chests and expect of them virtue and enterprise
We laugh at honour and are shocked to find traitors in our midst
We castrate and bid the geldings be fruitful

The Abolition of Man, Chapter 1, p. 704
The Complete C. S. Lewis Signature Classics

As they say, "You can't eat your cake and have it." Anyone could get caught in this rut; if not physically, at least mentally. He could be caught on either side; or at worst, on both sides as perpetrator and "perpetratee."

But wherever any precept of traditional morality
is simply challenged to produce its credentials
as though the burden of proof lay on it
we have taken the wrong position

The Abolition of Man, Chapter 2, p. 716
THE COMPLETE C. S. LEWIS SIGNATURE CLASSICS

Rational man can be quite irrational and proud in his pursuit of rationality. He quickly forgets that rationality is no panacea as history evidences. Vance Havner used to say that, "...man never had more artificial illumination and less true light. Bodily, he walks in unprecedented brilliance, while his soul dwells in unmitigated night. He can release a nuclear glory that out-dazzles the sun, and with it he plans his own destruction. He can put satellites in the sky, and left to himself, he is a wandering star to whom is reserved the blackness of darkness forever."

But the man-moulders of the new age will be armed with
powers of an omnicompetent state and an irresistible scientific technique...

The Abolition of Man, Chapter 3, p. 721
THE COMPLETE C. S. LEWIS SIGNATURE CLASSICS

Tim Lahaye refers to these man-moulders as "mind benders." Be wary when the state begins to play the role of an over-concerned parent or takes on the "power of attorney" over "embryonic" citizens. The collaboration of the state and so-called "experts" can birth and has birthed (consider Soviet Russia and China) much inhumanity against mankind.

Catherine Marshall

...money is really only ideas that have been converted
into a form usable in the exchange markets of earth

To Live Again, Chapter 4, p. 64
Catherine Marshall

Granted, money-making ideas could be good or evil. However, ideas cannot yield money until this conversion process occurs. What are you waiting for? Today is the best day to start penning those ideas that have been swirling in your mind. The next step is to act. Let the conversion process begin!

...the lonely person often makes the mistake of thinking
that physical nearness to other people is the answer
Yet some of the most solitary people in the world live in great cities...
One can feel utterly alone, have no sense of belonging
even in the midst of a jostling crowd

To Live Again, Chapter 7, p. 95
Catherine Marshall

Loneliness could be seen as the loss of meaningful exchange between a man and the other (beings, ideas and the likes). One can be physically alone without being lonely if productively engaged with the message from books or audio-visual recordings. This isn't to downplay the importance of physical proximity. It is still valuable, even if it occurs at low frequencies.

Don't make the mistake... of thinking
that the only lonely people are single people
Loneliness doesn't fly out the window in the wake of the marriage ceremony

To Live Again, Chapter 7, p. 95
Catherine Marshall

A word of caution to those who think that marriage is a panacea for loneliness. Many confuse wedding with marriage. A glamorous wedding can still lead to a marriage in doldrums. On the other hand, a solemn wedding can usher in one the best fusions of two humans on earth. Communication goes beyond physical proximity and speech. Two people whose hearts are miles from each other might still be sharing the same room.

The mold was broken when each of us was born

To Live Again, Chapter 7, p. 103
CATHERINE MARSHALL

This speaks to that uniqueness in every man. In a sense, God makes no duplicates. God sent you into this world to accomplish a specific assignment(s). Find it! Better still, complete it.

Charles Spurgeon

Prayer is the lisping of the believing infant
the shout of the fighting believer
the requiem of the dying saint falling asleep in Jesus

From Morning and Evening
Charles Spurgeon

Although prayer might vary in fervency and effectiveness, it is available to every "category" of believer. Today is the best day to start making effective use of prayer.

Chinese Saying

The palest ink lasts longer than the finest memory

Chinese Saying

Proper documentation preserves information better than our memories. One uniqueness of the human memory is its proclivity to distort information over time. What are you waiting for? Start penning those ideas.

Christian G. Weiss

Every earnest Christian seeking divine guidance
should read the whole Word of God from cover to cover
at least once once each year

The Perfect Will of God, Chapter X, p. 75
CHRISTIAN G. WEISS

So, if you really desire to know God's will
make the Word of God your constant companion
Know it better than you know anything else in this whole world

---

The Perfect Will of God, Chapter X, p. 76
CHRISTIAN G. WEISS

Many see personal, systematic Bible study as an uphill task. Well, what viable alternative do you have? Studying God's Word isn't a command tailor-made for the "bookish" and introverted Christian. Temperamental quirks are no excuses here. The Bible is called the "Manufacturer's Manual" by many for a reason. Now is the right time to design your yearly curriculum and to start reading God's Word.

Divine guidance must either come through
or in perfect harmony with the written Word of God
Anything else is not divine guidance

The Perfect Will of God, Chapter X, p. 80
CHRISTIAN G. WEISS

This is a sure safeguard against error. Discard any dream, vision, prophecy or counsel that fails this test; regardless of the spiritual credibility of its source(s).

Craig Groeschel

Addictions are idolatry

The Christian Atheist
CRAIG GROESCHEL

This might startle you at first. However, take some time to think it through. A man might never overcome addictions until he sees them for what they are. Isn't idolatry anything which trumps obedience to God's commands in your life?

D

Dag Hammarskjold
David Jordan
David McKay

Dag Hammarskjold

You cannot play with falsehood without forfeiting your right to truth
Or play with cruelty without losing your sensitivity of mind
He who wants to keep his garden tidy doesn't reserve a plot for weeds

DAG HAMMARSKJOLD

Many things in life are often demarcated by a chasm and not a fence. Thus, affording no room for straddlers and fence-sitters. Examples include truth and falsehood, good and evil, right and wrong. History provides ample evidence of the deadly consequences of muddling up these things.

David Jordan

> There is no real excellence in all this world
> which can be separated from right living

DAVID JORDAN

Excellence doesn't necessarily accompany success. Success could be achieved without right living; but excellence, never.

David McKay

The greatest battles of life
are fought out daily in the silent chambers of the soul

DAVID MCKAY

Your heart is your engine. Guard it like a fortress, which it is. Don't provide temporary shelter for any unworthy thought there.

E

E. M. Gray
Earl Paulk
Ella Wheeler Wilcox

E. M. Gray

The successful person
has the habit of doing the things failures don't like to do
They don't like doing them either
But their disliking is subordinated to the strength of their purpose

The Common Denominator of Success
E. M. GRAY

Your desire to succeed (in a good cause) must outweigh your dislike for the prerequisite work. The habitual practice of strength of purpose initiates and sustains success.

Earl Paulk

The true measure of success is the quality of our successors

Spiritual Megatrends, p. 281
EARL PAULK

Are you preparing the right people to continue from the height God has given in your lifetime? Are you big enough to empower them for leadership without getting in their way? This is quite a sobering thought for everyone: parents, leaders and mentors.

Ella Wheeler Wilcox

One ship drives east, and another drives west
with the self-same winds that blow
'Tis the set of the sails, and not the gales
which tells us the way they go
Like the waves of the sea are the ways of fate
as we voyage along thru' life
'Tis the set of the soul which decides its goal
and not the calm or the strife

ELLA WHEELER WILCOX

You don't and can't determine many circumstances in life. Examples include birthplace, parents and siblings. However, you can choose to make the best of these circumstances. You can decide to move in a better direction. The first step could be leaving the wrong crowd and befriending like-minded people. Your mindset determines your destination.

F

Francis Bacon

Francis Bacon

...all colors will agree in the dark

Essays or Counsels, Civil & Moral, III, Of Unity In Religion, p. 13
FRANCIS BACON, EDITED BY CLARK SUTHERLAND NORTHUP

Syncretism and its namesake ecumenism, have deadly undertones. God built variety into humans from the start. This is one reason why people with a fundamental unity in creed might have diverse ways of expressing it. Therefore, to achieve syncretism, there must needs be a smudging of all colors: even "black and white" become "indefinite shades of gray." Hence, truth (which is like light) becomes the sacrificial lamb and dissenting voices are made dumb.

Certainly, in taking revenge, a man is but even with his enemy
but in passing it over, he is superior; for it is a prince's part to pardon

---

Essays or Counsels, Civil & Moral, IV, Of Revenge, p. 15
FRANCIS BACON, EDITED BY CLARK SUTHERLAND NORTHUP

This is certain, that a man that studieth revenge
keeps his own wounds green which otherwise would heal and do well

---

Essays or Counsels, Civil & Moral, IV, Of Revenge, p. 16
FRANCIS BACON, EDITED BY CLARK SUTHERLAND NORTHUP

Forgiveness is healthy for the spirit, soul and body. It prevents psychosomatic illnesses and elevates you above your offenders.

...for prosperity doth best discover vice
but adversity doth best discover virtue

Essays or Counsels, Civil & Moral, V, Of Adversity, p. 17
FRANCIS BACON, EDITED BY CLARK SUTHERLAND NORTHUP

The depths of your vices will not surface until prosperity meets you. On the other hand, the shallowness of your virtues will not appear until adversity hits you.

Some books are to be tasted, others to be swallowed
and some few to be chewed and digested

Essays or Counsels, Civil & Moral, L, Of Studies, p. 155
Francis Bacon, Edited by Clark Sutherland Northup

Optimize your study time by arranging your to-read list in order of value.

Reading maketh a full man
conference a ready man
and writing an exact man

Essays or Counsels, Civil & Moral, L, Of Studies, p. 155
Francis Bacon, Edited by Clark Sutherland Northup

Although reading adds length, breath and depth to your life, it can bloat you with "mere" knowledge. However, discussing with others helps to sort your thoughts and puts your knowledge in perspective. Finally, writing down your thoughts for others to consider sharpens your thinking and increases the precision of your ideas.

G

G. Campbell Morgan
G. W. F. Hegel
Gary Friesen & Robin Maxon
Gary Thomas
George Seldes
Geothe
Glenn Clark
Gresham Machen

G. Campbell Morgan

Righteousness, apart from its relation to love, may do many cruel things

God's Perfect Will, p. 52
G. CAMPBELL MORGAN

A virtue taken to the extreme without the counterbalance of complementary virtue(s) becomes a vice. We need to carefully and daily examine our motives under the Light of God's Word.

. . . God does not call men away from the commonplaces of the busy days
but conditions their life within them
until the meanest thing flashes and gleams with the glory of the heavens

God's Perfect Will, p. 69
G. CAMPBELL MORGAN

We ought to live for Christ at all times. Guard against the hypocritical dichotomy between sacred and secular pursuits.

G. W. F. Hegel

What history teaches us is that men have never learned anything from it

G. W. F. Hegel

We have a natural propensity to think we're smarter than our predecessors. He who refuses to learn from the mistakes of others, should prepare to repeat them and accept the consequences.

Gary Friesen & Robin Maxon

Treat your Bible as if it were overflowing with God's Guidance — for it is

Decision Making & The Will of God, Chapter 3, p. 50
GARY FRIESEN & ROBIN MAXON

You can't go wrong by staying close to God's Word. The journey might take a while, but the road is never slippery.

Gary Thomas

A common mission is a powerful tool of marital intimacy

A Lifelong Love, Chapter 5, p. 93
GARY THOMAS

After all Amos 3:3 says, "Can two walk together, except they be agreed?" People who are yoked together can't make progress by heading in different directions. Sex is a physical tool of marital intimacy. However, trouble isn't far behind when it becomes the primary tool for intimacy in a marriage. Marital intimacy should be well-orbed and include other dimensions like emotional, mental and spiritual.

Marriage is a picture of the gospel before it is a vehicle of happiness
It's a prophetic call and duty before it is a playground of romanticism
It's a serious business, not a sentimental act of whimsy

A Lifelong Love, Chapter 8, p. 118
GARY THOMAS

This message is urgently needed today! No institution fulfils its vision when run by men who don't know the founder's intentions. The same applies to marriage. The right picture of marriage is discerned through careful study of Scriptures: weighing its role and significance in God's Grand Scheme. Isn't the rampant divorce and separation in the Church today traceable to wrong or faulty theology on marriage?

Holiness is the guardian of happiness, not its enemy

A Lifelong Love, Epilogue, p. 321
GARY THOMAS

If properly understood, holiness and happiness aren't mutually exclusive. Most virtues come in counterbalancing pairs or groups for a reason: to guard one another from being perverted into vices.

...if you make one bad financial investment, you can always start over
but biblical marriage is a one-shot deal

The Sacred Search, Chapter 1, p. 15
GARY THOMAS

This truth needs proper digestion in our generation. Isn't it sad to see divorce ravage the Church? One wonders how people who remarry after initiating the breakage of their marriage can call themselves Christians, i.e. Christ-like people? Personally, I don't see any sound biblical ground(s) for divorce and remarriage. One thing is for sure: adultery isn't the unforgivable sin. Interestingly, the Bible doesn't give detailed description of each man's "cross." However, the uniqueness of each "cross" is deducible from the teachings of Jesus Christ.

Some people may want to be married to you
but they may not have what it takes

The Sacred Search, Chapter 10, p. 117
GARY THOMAS

Refrain from marrying out of pity or for convenience. It can quickly degenerate into a lifelong nightmare. The reverse of this quote also holds. If that's your case, prayerfully start working on the missing ingredients before entering into marriage.

We live in a time when the word [covenant]
is all but absent in our vocabulary
It's interesting that the diminished use of this word
mirrors the increase of divorce both inside and outside the church

---

The Sacred Search: Couple's Conversation Guide, Session 3, p. 39
GARY THOMAS, STEVE WILKE & REBECCA WILKE

The divorce epidemic among unbelievers could be attributed to lack of grace which comes by saving faith. However, how do we explain the case within the Church? Is it a lack or failure of divinely approved leadership?

Is it symptomatic of an increase in false believers? Is it a pointer to a rise in shallow, lopsided and unbibilical theology?

God doesn't command you to get married
but once you choose to marry
He does intend for you to stay married

The Sacred Search: Couple's Conversation Guide, Session 3, p. 42
Gary Thomas, Steve Wilke & Rebecca Wilke

This applies to everyone: singles, married and separated. Singles (unmarried and widowed) who desire marriage ought to consider properly before stepping in. The separated (unofficial and official divorcees) ought to seek reconciliation. You know, I can't find any cogent biblical ground(s) for divorce. Also, let's remember that God is still the Ultimate Judge.

A holy couple, joined in marriage, can be a spiritual force
a God-oasis in a world that desperately needs spiritually strong people

The Sacred Search: Couple's Conversation Guide, Session 9, p. 120
Gary Thomas, Steve Wilke & Rebecca Wilke

Mark the words, "holy couple." The importance of holiness doesn't end after the wedding. It plays a vital role in marriage. "Pre-wedding" holiness ensures that little baggage is brought into the union. "Post-wedding" holiness helps maintain the union's sanity, sanctity and strength.

George Seldes

Fear is stronger than arms

The Great Thoughts
AESCHYLUS
IN GEORGE SELDES

Arms can hurt the body but not necessarily the mind. Fear on the other hand starts with the mind before getting to the body. Therefore, fear does more damage to a man than any external force.

United we stand, divided we fall

The Great Thoughts
AESOP
IN GEORGE SELDES

As much as this is true in principle, on what grounds should we stand? There are times when it's wise to divide on issues for conscience's sake.

The wise learn many things from their foes

The Great Thoughts
ARISTOPHANES
IN GEORGE SELDES

A wise man is humble enough to realise that he doesn't have all the answers. Therefore, he is willing to learn, even from unfair statements made by critics and antagonists. In fact, he might get new ideas this way. When was the last time you learnt anything from your opponents?

I count him braver who overcomes his desires
than him who conquers his enemies
for the hardest victory is the victory over self

The Great Thoughts
ARISTOTLE
IN GEORGE SELDES

If you doubt this, simply give it a try? We always underestimate the strength of those desires until they rise against our will.

Words are Weapons

The Great Thoughts
AUTHOR'S NATIVE VERMONT NEIGHBOR
IN GEORGE SELDES

On the other hand, words are balms. It all depends on the wielder. Are you wielding yours for good?

Remember that time is money

The Great Thoughts
BENJAMIN FRANKLIN
IN GEORGE SELDES

As much as possible, spend little to no time on worthless projects and pastimes. Spend time as you would spend hard-earned money.

Under the rule of the "Dollar" human life has fallen to its lowest value

---

The Great Thoughts
CHARLES AUGUSTUS LINDBERGH
IN GEORGE SELDES

The love of money has driven and still drives many into despicable deeds they once thought beneath their honour. It has a way of deadening a man's conscience, till he embraces the lie that everything has a price tag.

In the kingdom of the blind, the one-eyed man is the king

The Great Thoughts
DESIDERIUS ERASMUS
IN GEORGE SELDES

Don't take that little light of yours for granted. You never know the positive impacts it can have on others.

The easiest person to deceive is one's self

The Great Thoughts
EDWARD GEORGE BULWER-LYTTON
IN GEORGE SELDES

Hypocrisy is a scary thing. None truly knows himself in the entire sense. Keep careful watch over your life.

They that deny a God destroy men's nobility
for certainly man is kin to the beasts by his body
and if he be not kin to God by his spirit
he is a base and ignoble creature

The Great Thoughts
FRANCIS BACON
IN GEORGE SELDES

Isn't this still the situation today? Few believe the divine creation of man. Is it surprising when animal rights now take precedence over human rights? Many are blind to that divine spark within man's soul.

The ways to enrich are many and most of them foul

The Great Thoughts
FRANCIS BACON
IN GEORGE SELDES

You can't remain innocent for long by pursuing riches at all cost. Guide your determined pursuits with principles.

To stand still on the summit of perfection is difficult
and in the natural course of things, what cannot go forward slips back

The Great Thoughts
GAIUS VELLEIUS PATERCULUS
IN GEORGE SELDES

Stagnation is a dangerous; irrespective of the height at or from which it occurs. For one, determined minds might attain and exceed that height. You've effectually fallen behind when that happens. Nevertheless, comparing oneself with others isn't necessarily wise. Compare yourself to that potential God has given you.

Liberals have learned at a fearful cost
the lesson that absolute power corrupts absolutely
They have yet to learn that absolute liberality corrupts absolutely

The Great Thoughts
GERTRUDE HIMMELFARB
IN GEORGE SELDES

Life ought to be lived within the bounds of principles. Even compassion will birth tyranny when taken to the extreme. A boundary-less society soon devolves into anarchy. Similarly, a boundary-less life is soon spent.

Your son:
at five is your master
at ten your slave
at fifteen your double
and after that, your friend or foe
depending on his bringing up

The Great Thoughts
HASDAI IBN SHAPRUT
IN GEORGE SELDES

The results of child training might not be immediately obvious. They become glaring down the line. Be wary of these "experts" on child training who have no experience raising one themselves. Stick to those good old, time-tested principles. Notice how a child turns you into his slave in his initial helpless months. Few years later, the roles are reversed. You issue commands which he obeys: gladly or grudgingly. Then comes the troublesome teen years, and this is where many parents miss it. They refuse to adjust their parenting style from authoritarian to collegial. Unfortunately, this might be their last opportunity to directly influence the child for good.

In order to see Christianity, one must forget almost all Christians

---

The Great Thoughts
HENRI FREDERIC AMIEL
IN GEORGE SELDES

What a sad but eerily true statement. It behoves us Christians to live above this shameful reproach, through God's Grace. Our practice in life must match our profession of faith. Let's drop every hypocrisy.

One man with God is always in the majority

The Great Thoughts
JOHN KNOX
IN GEORGE SELDES

Evil can engulf a society to the point where the majority rejects the good. However, those are also times when the minority can boldly stand with God on the side of right.

To be an atheist requires an infinitely greater measure of faith
than to receive all great truths which atheism would deny

The Great Thoughts
JOSEPH ADDISON
IN GEORGE SELDES

Many atheists claim to be "faith-less" and boast of their rationality. They seem to discern a great chasm between faith and reason. The fact is that someone can make reason his object of faith. Maybe it's high time they revisited the evidence against atheism.

To teach is to learn twice

The Great Thoughts
JOSEPH JOUBERT
IN GEORGE SELDES

As they say, "Practice makes perfect." Although knowledge passes from teacher to learner during teaching, it is also reinforced in the teacher.

I cannot and will not cut my conscience to fit this year's fashion

---

The Great Thoughts
LILLIAN HELLMAN
IN GEORGE SELDES

Fashion is driven by fads and whims. Conscience ought to be based on principles that stand the test of time. Don't place too much emphasis on conforming to fashion. Build your life around principles. After all, trimming your conscience every year will steadily make you unrecognisable.

Chance favors the trained mind

The Great Thoughts
LOUIS PASTEUR
IN GEORGE SELDES

Preparation properly positions you against that unknown time at which opportunity will knock.

Great men are they
who see that spiritual is stronger than any material force
that thoughts rule the world

The Great Thoughts
RALPH WALDO EMERSON (PROGRESS OF CULTURE)
IN GEORGE SELDES

A food for thought to those who believe that man is completely a material being.

Character is that which can do without success

The Great Thoughts
RALPH WALDO EMERSON
IN GEORGE SELDES

Character and success are two different things. Not every successful person has the character to go with it. On the flip side, there are many everyday people with stellar characters. Character is an intrinsic quality that radiates from a man. It includes virtues like punctuality, honesty and integrity. Success is an external quality that could be as shallow as can be.

Parricide is more wicked than homicide, but suicide is most wicked of all

The Great Thoughts
SAINT AUGUSTINE
IN GEORGE SELDES

How many clearly speak this kind of truth today? In fact, we now have legal provisions to assist a person in suicide if he so wishes. Human life has become so devalued that self-murder is now a respectable choice.

Serving one's own passions is the greatest slavery

The Great Thoughts
THOMAS FULLER
IN GEORGE SELDES

Man wasn't designed to indulge every passing passion. Feelings have an awful way of deceiving a man into extreme subjectivism, until he finds it hard to live beyond himself.

The mob has many heads but no brains

The Great Thoughts
THOMAS FULLER
IN GEORGE SELDES

Mob mentality is no mentality, just sheer irrationality and disorder: and disorder can't suddenly produce order without a constructive force.

Moderation in temper is always a virtue
Moderation in principle is always a vice

The Great Thoughts
THOMAS PAINE
IN GEORGE SELDES

Be wary of the push for more "tolerance" today. Isn't it interesting how we can twist a word to suit our purposes? There is need for careful evaluation of ideas with respect to their possible and probable outworkings. There are many feel-good advisers out to trick you into selling your soul in a blink.

Geothe

Things which matter most
must never be at the mercy of things which matter least

GEOTHE

The first step is having the right scale of preference. There are opportunity costs to positively influencing present and future generations. These costs could be certain friends, hobbies, unhealthy foods and so on.

Glenn Clark

Never is progress achieved by the masses
Creation ever remains the task of the individual

GLENN CLARK

Most historical instances of remarkable progress show the masses as too heavy a load, too rowdy a crowd, and too large a size to forge a clear path. Instead, you find one great leader who toils unseen for many years before others caught his vision. Interestingly, these leaders aren't always far-fetched. Consider all those "plain" mothers whose wombs and hands have shaped men of renown; also, those fathers who have inspired and mentored many to greatness.

Gresham Machen

Material betterment has gone hand in hand with spiritual decline

Christianity & Liberalism, p. 18
GRESHAM MACHEN

Although this observation has stood the test of time, its hard for some to see it for its worth. Although prosperity is biblical, the same Bible warns of its dangers. We need to strike a healthy balance here. That being said, prosperity has a way of draining spiritual vitality.

All the ideas of Christianity might be discovered in some other religion yet there would be in that other religion no Christianity

Christianity & Liberalism, p. 70
GRESHAM MACHEN

Christians ought to deeply understand Christ's uniqueness as the Mediator between God and man. To the best of my knowledge, no other world religion makes this claim.

H

H. Norman Wright
Helen Keller

H. Norman Wright

Marriage is one of God's greatest schools of learning
— it can be a place where husband and wife are refined

The Premarital Counseling Handbook, Chapter 1, p. 9
H. NORMAN WRIGHT

See the next time your spouse is "acting up" as another opportunity for learning and growth. On your wedding day, you signed up for this lifelong class on Christian living and human relations. However, this is no license for insensitivity and selfishness in marriage.

Helen Keller

Security does not exist in nature
Life is either a daring adventure or nothing at all

HELEN KELLER

There is no arrival port in life before it ends. So, take its ups and downs in good humour. Make the best of your short stay on earth.

J

J. Allan Petersen (Editor)
J. C. Ryle
James Allen
James Dobson
James Snyder
Janet Lowe
John Bunyan
John MacArthur
John Maxwell
John G. Paton
Joseph Milner

J. Allan Petersen (Editor)

…no nation has ever survived the disintegration of its home life

The Marriage Affair, p. 2
J. ALLAN PETERSEN (EDITOR)

A nation is built one home at a time. Is it any wonder we're headed for chaos when most bills passed into laws discourage home building and family life? How much lower can we sink than when political parties run on the promise of pro-choice options? One of such options being the lawful sanction to kill one's unborn babies or even oneself if one wishes. Why shouldn't a nation that degrades and devalues human life this much disintegrate? Please feel free to send your views across if you disagree.

The life of the mature person reveals a willingness to change
he is not content with mediocrity
and he believes "good enough" is not enough

The Marriage Affair, p. 7
J. ALLAN PETERSEN (EDITOR)

Maturity comes with a great degree of humility: a willingness to admit wrong and change stance. Also, it doesn't mean being "well cooked;" since more cooking will damage that person. Instead, maturity can be seen as a progressive realization of the weakness of your strengths, the strength of your weaknesses, and the increasing willingness to deal with them.

The child is like a seismograph
It registers every domestic earthquake and every marital shock

The Marriage Affair, p. 10
J. ALLAN PETERSEN (EDITOR)

Little wonder many young adults are and will be morally and psychologically bankrupt. We've reached the point of redefining gender and marriage (a feat to the best of my knowledge that previous civilizations didn't attempt or achieve for good reasons). Only God will help future generations surmount the mess we're creating. Marriage is increasingly becoming a power-play between selfish spouses. None pauses long enough to genuinely take the child's well-being into consideration. All the clamour for more child-rights is a mirage. Actually, I think it's a push for the destruction of men, through the deception of women, and for the eventual confusion of children.

Thus, when a home is destroyed
God loses one of the greatest theological seminaries in the world...

The Marriage Affair, p. 11
J. Allan Petersen (Editor)

This requires deep meditation today when many so-called "Christian" homes are breaking due to divorce. It's actually a disgrace that brings contempt on God's name. I leave you with this gnawing question: is there any cogent biblical ground(s) for divorce?

Males are born, but men are made

The Marriage Affair, p. 65
J. Allan Petersen (Editor)

Although you didn't choose how you were born, you can decide to remain a boyish man or a mature man. Manhood isn't necessarily attained with age. Start working on it today.

Love without discipline is pure sentiment. Discipline without love is tyranny

---

The Marriage Affair, p. 127
J. Allan Petersen (Editor)

All forms of discipline
to be successful must be based on the foundation of love

The Marriage Affair, p. 171
J. Allan Petersen (Editor)

Even virtues have boundaries. Parents who so much love their children at the expense of disciplining them will eventually deliver narcissistic ego-maniacs to the society. Similarly, parents who so much discipline their children without love will eventually deliver psychopathic sociopaths to the society. There needs to be a tenuous balance of love and discipline in child training; or in any human relationship for that matter.

A Christ-like example
is the greatest educational influence in the lives of our children

---

The Marriage Affair, p. 129
J. ALLAN PETERSEN (EDITOR)

Hypocrisy in a parent's life is deadly: to parent and child. Now is a good time for parents and leaders to evaluate their Christ-likeness.

... parenthood is a full-time job...

The Marriage Affair, p. 138
J. ALLAN PETERSEN (EDITOR)

The most rigorous job in the world is being a parent

The Marriage Affair, p. 165
J. ALLAN PETERSEN (EDITOR)

Parenthood is actually more than a job. It is a divine assignment and mission. Don't be so eager to evangelize nations at the neglect of those God has placed under your care.

There is more to being a father than bringing home a paycheck

---

The Marriage Affair, p. 148
J. ALLAN PETERSEN (EDITOR)

Money doesn't, hasn't and can't turn a man into a father. One food for thought: do you live according to godly principles worthy of emulation by your children and society at large?

J. C. Ryle

Let us never forget that truth
distorted and exaggerated
can become the mother of the most dangerous heresies

Holiness — It's Nature, Hindrances, Difficulties and Roots
Introduction, p. 11
J. C. RYLE

Never leave wisdom behind in your zealous pursuit. Don't go beyond the bounds of truth. Just because it is truth doesn't mean it is boundless.

A regeneration which a man can have
and yet live carelessly in sin or worldliness
is a regeneration invented by uninspired theologians
but never mentioned in Scripture

Holiness — It's Nature, Hindrances, Difficulties and Roots
Chapter II, p. 32
J. C. RYLE

Beware of those preachers who stray from Scriptures. Wisely keep your distance despite their sincerity and eloquence. How can a man claim to be regenerated with no visible change in lifestyle?

The notion of a purgatory after death which shall turn sinners into saints
is a lying invention of man and is nowhere taught in the Bible
We must be saints before we die, if we are to be saints afterwards in glory

Holiness — It's Nature, Hindrances, Difficulties and Roots
Chapter II, p. 42
J. C. RYLE

There is an urgent need to prioritize the reading of the entire Scriptures at least once a year. This should guard you against pedlars of false doctrine. Remember that God has the final say irrespective of our convictions on earth. Please ensure that your faith is on firm foundation.

Christ will never be found the Saviour of those
who know nothing of following His example

Holiness — It's Nature, Hindrances, Difficulties and Roots
Chapter II, p. 37
J. C. RYLE

That eventual "Salvation" in the afterlife will reveal those who truly trusted and followed Christ on earth. There are many whose preaching and practice are so inconsistent and distorted to the point they appear to perfect hypocrisy instead of holiness.

To reach the holiday of glory
we must pass through the training school of grace

Holiness — It's Nature, Hindrances, Difficulties and Roots
Chapter III, p. 58
J. C. RYLE

Although God is Love, He doesn't approve of all men's deeds. The life a man lives on earth has eternal consequences. Don't expect to enter Heaven in the afterlife without proper preparation in this life.

Private religion must receive our first attention, if we wish our souls to grow

Holiness — It's Nature, Hindrances, Difficulties and Roots
Chapter VI, p. 101
J. C. RYLE

A man's life could be unpleasant to God despite his frequent display of and attendance to public religion. Salvation and grace are personal gifts from God meant for the Church's edification. Since the Church comprises individuals, these gifts are actually meant for mutual edification. How then can a Church thrive with malnourished members? One needs to prioritize his private devotion: prayer, study, praise, meditation and the rest. Public religion can't and shouldn't be as substitute for private religion.

We must aim to have a Christianity which, like the sap of a tree
runs through every twig and leaf of our character, and sanctifies all

Holiness — It's Nature, Hindrances, Difficulties and Roots
Chapter VI, p. 101
J. C. RYLE

This is a call to stand against hypocrisy: not just any hypocrisy, but self-hypocrisy. Today is the right and best time to re-evaluate your Christianity and ensure that it is one seamless continuum in private and public.

Disease is infectious, but health is not
... Mistakes in friendship or marriage-engagements
are the whole reason why some have entirely ceased to grow

Holiness — It's Nature, Hindrances, Difficulties and Roots
Chapter VI, p. 102
J. C. RYLE

Be very deliberate in choosing your close acquaintances. It is easier for evil to negatively influence good than for good to positively influence evil. Marriage is one key relationship that demands careful consideration long before entry. Carefully think this one over.

Let us never measure our religion by that of others
and think we are doing enough if we have gone beyond our neighbours...
Let us follow on
making Christ's life and character our only pattern and example

Holiness — It's Nature, Hindrances, Difficulties and Roots
Chapter VI, p. 106
J. C. RYLE

God gave everyone a unique set of gifts. Hence, it is kind of unwise to compare yourself with others. Also, man is fallible. Hence, we ought to compare ourselves to Christ, our perfect standard; who lived infallibly on earth as the Son of Man.

It is good sometimes to be kept waiting
we do not value things which we get without trouble

Holiness — It's Nature, Hindrances, Difficulties and Roots
Chapter VII, p. 133
J. C. RYLE

God is no genie, neither is prayer some kind of magic. Prayers are answered in the way best suited to God's Design. Waiting could be His present answer and a paying proposition for us. I don't think I'm as grateful to God for those things I easily get compared to those which cost me a lot. Well, we all need to work on it.

Spiritual darkness comes on horseback, and goes away on foot

Holiness — It's Nature, Hindrances, Difficulties and Roots
Chapter VII, p. 133
J. C. RYLE

Evil might be unheralded when it comes for surveillance. However, its invasion into the life of a man or society is usually attended with much pomp and pageantry. On the other hand, its eviction requires a lot of opposition and patience. It seldom makes haste to leave, even when it has to do so in disgrace. Be very careful of any evil you excuse today. It might claim a lawful right over you tomorrow.

The eye of the child drinks in far more than the ear
A child will always observe what you do much more than what you say

---

Holiness — It's Nature, Hindrances, Difficulties and Roots
Chapter IX, p. 169
J. C. RYLE

This is an important message for parents, leaders and teachers. Your life is the best lesson you can prepare for a child. Watch over your life and you're half-way done with child training.

He that would be conformed to Christ's image and become a Christ-like man must be constantly studying Christ Himself

---

Holiness — It's Nature, Hindrances, Difficulties and Roots
Chapter XII, p. 204
J. C. RYLE

Challenge anything which prevents you from doing this. It could be legitimate things that are religious, economic, educational and so on.

The harvest of the Lord's field is seldom ripened by sunshine only
It must go through its days of wind, and rain, and storm

Holiness — It's Nature, Hindrances, Difficulties and Roots
Chapter XII, p. 206
J. C. Ryle

The work of God isn't all smooth-sailing. It often comprises long periods of opposition and trouble mingled with calm interludes. Tests and trials are part of the curriculum in God's School.

Human nature is always the same in every age

Holiness — It's Nature, Hindrances, Difficulties and Roots
Chapter XVII, p. 270
J. C. Ryle

History shows that education and culture can refine human behaviour without disturbing his core nature.

When you cannot answer a sceptic, be content to wait for more light
but never forsake a great principle

Holiness — It's Nature, Hindrances, Difficulties and Roots
Chapter XIX, p. 294
J. C. Ryle

What a word of caution to the Christian! Don't quickly jettison a time-tested principle because you have no ready-made answers for those who question it. Rather, take it as an opportunity to genuinely "re-evaluate" your convictions on that principle. If it's truly a principle, you will discover better reasons to hold it tighter.

A Bible-reading laity is a nation's surest defence against error

Holiness — It's Nature, Hindrances, Difficulties and Roots
Chapter XIX, p. 299
J. C. Ryle

The Bible in the pulpit must never supersede the Bible at home

Holiness — It's Nature, Hindrances, Difficulties and Roots
Chapter XIX, p. 304
J. C. Ryle

It is bad for a spiritual leader to so emphasize public worship to the detriment of personal and family devotion. Here is one good reason. A pulpit is mounted by a fallible man and can therefore quickly become a fountain of error.

James Allen

...we will find what we seek for
only by patience, practice, and ceaseless importunity

As a Man Thinketh, p. 8
JAMES ALLEN

Notice the elements of time and effort in this combination. Effort alone isn't always enough and time alone is wishful thinking.

The human mind may be likened to a garden
which may be intelligently cultivated or allowed to run wild
But whether cultivated or neglected, it must and will bring forth

As a Man Thinketh, p. 9
JAMES ALLEN

Now is the best and right time to start cultivating your mind.

The soul attracts that which it secretly harbors

As a Man Thinketh, p. 11
JAMES ALLEN

As we think, so we are; as we continue to think, so we remain

As a Man Thinketh, p. 31
JAMES ALLEN

A man can rise no higher than his state of mind. Stop visualizing negativity while confessing positivity. Your subconscious doesn't know any better. It unquestioningly accepts the internal data as fact irrespective of your external display.

The child cries to be a man or woman
the man and woman sigh for the lost felicity of childhood

From Poverty to Power, Part 1, The Lesson of Evil
JAMES ALLEN

Let's learn to be content in our current situation and make the best of it. As they say, "The grass is always greener on the other side."

The foolish wish and grumble; the wise work and wait

From Poverty to Power, Part 1, The Secret To Health, Success and Power
JAMES ALLEN

Wishful thinking has never solved any problem; neither has grumbling. Accepting responsibility is a good step towards addressing problems. Start today by doing something about it. Don't forget that patient waiting is part of the package if there are little results at first.

The heights by great men reached and kept
Were not attained by sudden flight
But they, while their companions slept
Were toiling upward in the night

From Poverty to Power, Part 2, The Power of Meditation
JAMES ALLEN

Consider these key points: height attainment and height maintenance. None is achieved without patience and dedicated effort. Although effort alone might not be sufficient, it is still an important factor for success. As Bill Newman said, "overnight success is a myth."

Men and women of real power and influence are few because
few are prepared to make the sacrifice necessary to the acquisition of power
and fewer still are ready to patiently build up character

From Poverty to Power, Part 2, The Acquisition of Spiritual Power
JAMES ALLEN

There are two things here: real power and influence on one hand; sacrifice, patience and character on the other. These are like two legs which keep us in balance. History is replete with the catastrophe caused by men who wielded great power and influence with little character. Interestingly, character cannot be purchased or loaned. It is built through tests, trials and time.

That only can be called reform which tends to reform the human heart
for all evil has its rise there...

From Poverty to Power, Part 2, The Realization of Selfless Love
JAMES ALLEN

As someone said, "The heart of the matter is the matter of the heart." Governments and society have tried with reasonable success to polish man's personality but have woefully failed to affect his character. Is it then strange, that the more refined a civilization gets, the more refined its evils get? Civilization isn't the answer. Education might help but isn't the answer. A life-changing power which transcends the mundane is needed. I present the God-Man, Jesus Christ, as the answer. Please consider this proposition in light of the evidence before walking away.

Truth is nothing if not unchangeable...

From Poverty to Power, Part 2, Saints, Sages and Saviors
JAMES ALLEN

Some say we now live in a post-truth, post-modern culture. Well, I don't know about that. If this is an excuse to say that truth is relative, we really need to weigh the evidence. I'm no philosopher. My humble understanding is that truth can be likened to a lighthouse used to estimate one's bearing while out on this troubled sea of life. If that lighthouse is also adrift, what sense of direction is left?

James Dobson

A personal relationship with Jesus Christ is the cornerstone of marriage
giving meaning and purpose to every dimension of living

Stories of the Heart and Home, p. 82
JAMES DOBSON

Being able to bow in prayer as the day begins or ends
gives expression to the frustrations and concerns
that might not otherwise be ventilated

Stories of the Heart and Home, p. 82
JAMES DOBSON

Every troubled teen should be so fortunate as to have parents
who are still pulling for him and praying for him and feeling for him
even when he has become most unlovable

Stories of the Heart and Home, p. 83
JAMES DOBSON

This should forearm the unmarried who are seeking marriage. Also, it should encourage the married who are experiencing some challenges with their children or spouse at home.

The essential investment of commitment
is sorely missing in so many modern marriages
...Sooner or later, this unanchored love will certainly vaporize

Stories of the Heart and Home, p. 95
JAMES DOBSON

Simply put, the stability of marriage
is a by-product of an iron-willed determination to make it work
If you choose to marry, enter into that covenant
with the resolve to remain committed to each other for life
Never threaten to leave your mate in angry moments
Don't allow yourself to consider the possibility of divorce
Calling it quits must not be an option for those who want to go the distance!

Stories of the Heart and Home, p. 115
JAMES DOBSON

Many marry without a balanced understanding of love and marriage. Marriage is the yoking of two unique lives to form one unique unit. This yoking eliminates or curtails some old freedoms and provides or guarantees new ones. A mindset change is needed while entering marriage and a daily mindset renewal is needed in the marriage to sustain it.

James Snyder

The best repentance is to do it no more

The Life of A. W. Tozer: In Pursuit of God, p. 12
JAMES SNYDER

One of the keys to right living is ensuring that your words correspond to your actions. This safeguards you against hypocrisy.

Janet Lowe

Even if it were desirable
America is not strong enough to police the world by military force
If that attempt is made
the blessings of liberty will be replaced by tyranny and coercion at home
Our Christian ideals cannot be exported to other lands by dollars and guns
Persuasion and example
are the methods taught by the Carpenter of Nazareth
and if we believe in Christianity
we should try to advance our ideals by his methods

Warren Buffett Speaks, p. 41
HOWARD BUFFETT
IN JANET LOWE

This warning still holds true today: for Christians, leaders and the world at large. The "...end does not always justify the means" and the "...means determines the end."

John Bunyan

Temptations when we meet them at first
are as the lion that roared upon Samson
But if we overcome them, the next time we see them
we shall find a nest of honey within them

Grace Abounding to the Chiefest Of Sinners
JOHN BUNYAN

As they say, "Practice makes perfect." This is also applicable in the spiritual. Don't just throw in your towel. Keep standing against temptation and sin.

John MacArthur

Truth without love has no decency; it's just brutality
On the other hand, love without truth has no character; it's just hypocrisy

Twelve Ordinary Men
JOHN MACARTHUR

Many virtues are interlinked for several reasons. A virtue quickly turns into a vice when taken to an extreme without the counterbalance of other virtues. I'm not talking about moderation here. The moderation which many practice is just "masked" hypocrisy since it doesn't always stand straight in matters of principle. The proper application of virtue is our consideration here. Don't pick and choose among virtues. Take all of them.

Ambition without humility becomes egotism

Twelve Ordinary Men
JOHN MACARTHUR

Today, many are so ambitious that they are willing to knock down anything standing in their way: be it spouse, children, parents, friends. This could be attributed to wrong priorities.

John Maxwell

Thinking is hard work; that's why so few do it

How Successful People Think
ALBERT EINSTEIN
IN JOHN MAXWELL

If you believe productive thinking is simple, why not give it a try?

Every tradition may not be a good idea for the future

How Successful People Think
ANDY STANLEY
IN JOHN MAXWELL

However, ponder hard and long before dropping any tradition. Many have destroyed themselves due to senseless pursuit of novelty.

He that is taught only by himself has a fool for a master

How Successful People Think
BEN JOHNSON
IN JOHN MAXWELL

Everyone has blind sides that can only be revealed by someone else. One remains perfect in his own eyes until he interacts with others. Human interaction has a way of rudely awaking us to our spots and blemishes.

We cannot hold a torch to light another's path without brightening our own

How Successful People Think
BEN SWEETLAND
IN JOHN MAXWELL

The help you sincerely give to others is never lost. It returns in so many ways.

Be ashamed to die until you have won some victory for humanity

How Successful People Think
HORACE MANN
IN JOHN MAXWELL

Don't just exist in this world. Make every single day memorable for good. Leave a remarkable trail.

The value of life lies not in the length of days
but in the use we make of them
a man may live long yet live very little

How Successful People Think
MICHEL EYQUEM DE MONTAIGNE
IN JOHN MAXWELL

Vance Havner once said that, "We've learned how to lengthen life, but we don't know how to deepen it." How are you living? Live as though you will account for how you spent today come dawn tomorrow.

Until thought is linked with purpose there is no intelligent accomplishment

How Successful People Think
JAMES ALLEN
IN JOHN MAXWELL

Aimless thinking is like a mad dog on the loose. It does much harm and little good. Guard and channel your thoughts properly.

Learning to write is learning to think
You don't know anything clearly unless you can state it in writing

How Successful People Think
S. I. HAYAKAWA
IN JOHN MAXWELL

A picture in your mind does good to none else. In fact, it might do you little good. Birth your thoughts into reality by penning them. There is an element of clarity and materialisation that comes with it.

Our society finds truth too strong a medicine to digest undiluted

How Successful People Think
TED KOPPEL
IN JOHN MAXWELL

Many pay lip service to the pursuit of truth. Be wary of the media, most best-sellers and popular culture.

The value of a good idea is in using it

How Successful People Think
THOMAS EDISON
IN JOHN MAXWELL

If you have an idea, don't keep it lying fallow. An idea yields nothing until it's tested.

It is hard to see the picture while inside the frame

How Successful People Think
JOHN MAXWELL

Distancing yourself from an issue and its surrounding constraints gives you a clearer perspective of the best course of action.

The mind will not focus until it has clear objectives

How Successful People Think
JOHN MAXWELL

Stop confusing your mind with dissonant visions. Sharpen your vision of the destination before embarking on the mission.

What are you giving up to go up?

How Successful People Think
JOHN MAXWELL

Excellence requires sacrifice. A man shouldn't expect to break new grounds without leaving his current situation. There is always an opportunity cost.

When was the last time you did something for the first time?

How Successful People Think
JOHN MAXWELL

Try new things. You never can tell what doors might open. Step out of your comfort zone once in while.

Men give me credit for genius; but all the genius I have lies in this when I have a subject on hand I study it profoundly

---

Talent Is Never Enough
ALEXANDER HAMILTON
IN JOHN MAXWELL

Talent without diligence eventually grows dull. Diligence sharpens talent into an irresistible arrow head.

We are what we repeatedly do. Excellence, then, is not an act but a habit

---

Talent Is Never Enough
ARISTOTLE
IN JOHN MAXWELL

Greatness lies in doing little things in a great way over time. It doesn't happen overnight.

Always make your learning greater than your experience

Talent Is Never Enough
CATHERINE NOMURA
IN JOHN MAXWELL

Life is larger than your experience. Sole reliance on personal experience without constant learning will cage you in the reality of your past.

The world stands aside to let anyone pass
who knows where he or she is going

Talent Is Never Enough
DAVID STAR JORDAN
IN JOHN MAXWELL

Not everyone on a mission towards progress has a vision of their destination. So, create a clear vision of your goal today. If you have, please confirm that it's still your desired target. Finally, chart a clear mission.

You cannot kindle a fire in any other heart
until it is burning within your own

Talent Is Never Enough
ELEANOR DOAN
IN JOHN MAXWELL

In other words, a man cannot give what he doesn't have. Transform yourself before helping others transform themselves. As William Gurnall said, "...charity may begin at home, though it must not end at home."

In every triumph there is a lot of try

Talent Is Never Enough
FRANK TYGER
IN JOHN MAXWELL

Never give up in the first few times you try. Seldom do people achieve any goal in one try.

The more you sweat in peace, the less you bleed in war

Talent Is Never Enough
GENERAL DOUGLASS MACARTHUR
IN JOHN MAXWELL

The skills needed for present success are usually acquired and honed in the past. Never belittle the value of those daily drills.

Bravery is the capacity to perform properly even when scared half to death

Talent Is Never Enough
General Omar Bradley
in John Maxwell

Bravery doesn't necessarily mean the absence of fear. It is the power to act despite the fear.

Few men have virtue enough to withstand the highest bidder

Talent Is Never Enough
George Washington
in John Maxwell

True virtue is stronger than any bribe or monetary enticement. It has always been a scarce commodity.

The man who has no inner life is the slave of his surroundings

Talent Is Never Enough
Henri Fredric Amiel
in John Maxwell

There is freedom in purposeful silence. Talkativeness is like a leak in the soul of a man. Speech has a way of diluting meditative prowess.

A belief is something you will argue about
A conviction is something you will die for

Talent Is Never Enough
Howard Hendricks
in John Maxwell

Conviction is belief at maturity. This is what ignites and strengthens a heart despite the approaching flames. Unfortunately, not every belief will mature into conviction.

He who has done his best for his own time
has lived for all times

Talent Is Never Enough
JOHANN VON SCHILLER
IN JOHN MAXWELL

Your lifespan on earth is finite. However, the way you live it has an infinite dimension. Your deeds, or at least their consequences have eternal ramifications. Live right, live well.

Talent can be cultivated in tranquility
Character only in the rushing stream of life

Talent Is Never Enough
JOHANN WOLFGANG VON GEOTHE
IN JOHN MAXWELL

Talent can be honed in the comfort of isolation. However, character must be developed and tested over and over in the furnace of human relationships. Many who have talent are sadly without character. Many with solid character have little talent. However, it is always a beauty to watch talented people with a solid character base.

Success bases our worth on a comparison with others
Excellence gauges our value by measuring us against our own potential

---

Talent Is Never Enough
JOHN JOHNSTON
IN JOHN MAXWELL

Success is an external measure of a man's worth. Excellence is a measure of a man's growth relative to his intrinsic potential. Hence, excellence is a better measure of worth. Success seldom comes with excellence. However, excellence often comes with success. Therefore pursue excellence; and you might get success thrown in.

It is what you learn after you know it all that counts

Talent Is Never Enough
JOHN WOODEN
IN JOHN MAXWELL

Humility is a virtue which none outgrows for good. Education (not just schooling) ought to be a life-long pursuit.

Make each day your masterpiece

Talent Is Never Enough
John Wooden
in John Maxwell

Don't dwell on yesterday's achievements or frustrations. Focus on how you can make today your best day yet.

There is no pillow as soft as a clear conscience

Talent Is Never Enough
John Wooden
in John Maxwell

A man may deaden his conscience for a while. However, it will catch up with him. Why take this chance in the first place?

It's good to celebrate and even take a rest but not for long
We must close the door on yesterday's success

Talent Is Never Enough
Lester Woerner
in John Maxwell

Today's success can be a major obstacle to achieving tomorrow's. Today's success is already ageing. Don't dwell much on it.

If a man hasn't discovered something that he will die for, He isn't fit to live

---

Talent Is Never Enough
Martin Luther King Jr.
in John Maxwell

A man without a vision large enough to demand his whole life will gradually drift into aimlessness.

What you focus on expands

Talent Is Never Enough
MIKE KENDRICK
IN JOHN MAXWELL

Never expect clarity of goals through diffuse concentration. The mind works best when given clear instructions. Don't clutter it with things you're unwilling to birth.

The Will must be stronger than the Skill

Talent Is Never Enough
MUHAMMAD ALI
IN JOHN MAXWELL

Skill has its place. However, a skilful man without the wilful mind eventually loses to someone with less skill and plenty will. Evaluate yourself right away!

Persistence is stubbornness with a purpose

Talent Is Never Enough
RICH DE VOSS
IN JOHN MAXWELL

Persistence has an element of purposeful stubbornness. It keeps a man grounded after many have long quit. How persistent are you in things that matter? You may need to start honing this skill today.

A character standard is far more important than even a gold standard

---

Talent Is Never Enough
ROGER BABASON
IN JOHN MAXWELL

What a truth we to practise more in our generation! Fame and fortune are transient and have their proper places. However, they can't sustain a society for long. Gold is an ephemeral substance which lures men into vice and vileness more often than not. On the other hand, character is ageless.

In life or in football
touchdowns rarely take place in seventy-yard increments
Usually it's three yards and a cloud of dust

Talent Is Never Enough
RUSH LIMBAUGH
IN JOHN MAXWELL

It's the little, unnoticeable things in life that accumulate to become the big, noticeable things. Don't skip any necessary step in life, irrespective of its seeming insignificance at the time.

There are many things that will catch my eye
but there are only a few that catch my heart
It is those I consider to pursue

Talent Is Never Enough
TIM REDMOND
IN JOHN MAXWELL

Be deliberate in filtering what you commit to. Don't get carried away by every new fad in town. Train your eyes to selectively discard interesting but unprofitable ventures.

It's the start that often stops people

Talent Is Never Enough
TIM REDMOND
IN JOHN MAXWELL

There is no harm in trying out something worthwhile. Don't wait until every variable falls in place; because it might never happen. Simply take that calculated risk!

All problems become smaller if you don't dodge them, but confront them
Touch a thistle timidly, and it pricks you;
grasp it boldly, and its spines crumble

Talent Is Never Enough
WILLIAM HALSEY
IN JOHN MAXWELL

There is a miracle in boldness, when rightly used. It is synonymous with faith to an extent. Boldness approaches obstacles with an irresistible force. Don't procrastinate problem solving. Boldly address them as soon as possible.

Quality is a race with no finish line

Talent Is Never Enough
WILLIAM JOHNSON
IN JOHN MAXWELL

Once you stop growing, you start stunting. Always compare yourself to your potential and not necessarily to others. I don't think any man ever exhausted his potential in his lifetime.

A passionate person with limited talent
will outperform a passive person who possesses greater talent

Talent Is Never Enough
JOHN MAXWELL

Talent and diligence are key ingredients of success. One without the other is handicapped. A lazy, talented person or a talented, lazy person is a pitiful sight. Laziness is like soot on the shining gem of talent.

In prosperity our friends know us
In adversity we know our friends

Talent Is Never Enough
JOHN MAXWELL

A friend that hasn't been tested can't be truly tested. Prosperity has a way of advertising a man to the world. Adversity has a way of revealing how a man's acquaintances value him.

Some people say that they feel burned out
The truth is that they probably never were on fire in the first place

Talent Is Never Enough
JOHN MAXWELL

The primary characteristic of fire is to burn. However, we need to strike a balance here. After a while, a man might need rest despite the fire (drive for goals) burning within him. However, there are many who burn themselves out through worry and doing work they have little passion for. If you're in this trap, start thinking of changing vocation.

If you are preparing today, chances are, you will not be repairing tomorrow

Talent Is Never Enough
JOHN MAXWELL

Anticipate what you need tomorrow and start working towards it today. It might be as simple as conditioning your mind. Build a foundation that's solid enough to carry that edifice. Else by tomorrow, you will retrogress by being bogged down with preventable breakdowns.

Developing talent without developing character is a dead end

Talent Is Never Enough
JOHN MAXWELL

Talent without character eventually defeats itself. Time will slowly but surely peel off the mask of impressions and reveal a man's character. Conversely, character without talent might not burn so bright; but it will guide a man steadily to his destination.

Talent without initiative never reaches its potential

Talent Is Never Enough
JOHN MAXWELL

Talent is like money. You cannot help yourself or others if it isn't spent. Spend your talent today. Take the first step of faith.

The wise man does at once what the fool does finally

Talent Is Never Enough
JOHN MAXWELL

Procrastination fools you into living today's life tomorrow. It does this by occupying you with unimportant or unproductive tasks today. Be deliberate in promptly executing your responsibilities.

Great souls have will but feeble ones have only wishes

Talent Is Never Enough
JOHN MAXWELL

It's easier to move from failure to success than from excuses to success

Talent Is Never Enough
JOHN MAXWELL

You won't make much impact in your generation until you graduate from "wishing" for achievement to "willing" to take responsibility for working towards your goals.

John G. Paton

Life is God's great gift, to be preserved for His uses, not thrown away

The Autobiography Of The Pioneer Missionary
To The New Hebrides, p. 108
JOHN G. PATON

Suicide, euthanasia, abortion and the likes are just murder's prettier sisters. They have no biblical ground(s).

The Pillar of Cloud and Fire still marches before us; but, alas how many have lost the power to behold it!

The Autobiography Of The Pioneer Missionary
To The New Hebrides, p. 483
JOHN G. PATON

This is the time to pray for the power to perceive these Pillars, maintain our gaze and march accordingly.

Joseph Milner

... but real Christians should have more in view than their own Salvation
— namely, the propagation of godliness to posterity

The History of the Church: Vol. I, Century One, Chapter XIV, p. 79
JOSEPH MILNER

What a challenge to leaders, parents, and mentors! Don't leave the next generation worse than yours. This calls for a deliberate investment of time, resource and effort: through prayer, counsel, encouragement and exemplary living.

The love of the world increases with the abatement of persecution

The History of the Church: Vol. I, Century One, Chapter XIV, p. 82-83
JOSEPH MILNER

Adversity has a way of helping us set our priorities right. There are many worldly things Christians excuse to accommodate their fancy and pleasure. They forget that the Scriptures are to be obeyed irrespective of our feelings, socio-economic status and prevalent societal conditions.

In all ages, men even of amiable morals, if destitute of true holiness are enemies of the Gospel

The History of the Church: Vol. I, Century Two, Chapter I, p. 131
JOSEPH MILNER

This doesn't mean that moral heathens should be despised. It is showing us that mere morality is not the Gospel's ultimate goal. Christian morality is usually the outworking of the in-working of holiness. After all, history records several moral philosophers who found reasons for abusing

Christ and Christians.

Humility is the guard of real Christian goodness

____

The History of the Church: Vol. I, Century Two, Chapter I, p. 137
JOSEPH MILNER

Pride is a natural propensity common to all men. If you don't rise against it daily, even your sacrificial giving becomes offensive before God and man.

Sagacious and holy men are never more apt to be deceived
than when they attempt to look into futurity

____

The History of the Church: Vol. I, Century Three, Chapter XII, p. 356
JOSEPH MILNER

Prophecy is a gift from God. However, it could could lead to disgrace if uncircumscribed by humility and wisdom.

Talents and learning are coveted by mankind
He, however, who possesses much of them has the more abundant need
to learn humility and divine caution

____

The History of the Church: Vol. I, Century Three, Chapter XV, p. 402
JOSEPH MILNER

As John Bunyan said, "He that is down need fear no fall; He that is low, no pride..." This is a warning to Christians who are rich in gifts. They ought to pray for the graces to match their gifts.

Sin is the real disease of mankind

____

The History of the Church: Vol. I, Century Three, Chapter XVI, p. 404
JOSEPH MILNER

This is a truth with strong historical evidence. Governmental interventions and societal reforms haven't been able to rid man of sin.

Indiscriminate incredulity is as blind as indiscriminate belief

---

The History of the Church: Vol. I, Century Three, Chapter XVI, p. 405
JOSEPH MILNER

A healthy dose of scepticism is needed for sanity and safety in life.

It has been the fashion to extol the moral part of the Scripture
I fear, with an insidious eye to the doctrinal

The History of the Church: Vol. I, Century Three, Chapter XXI, p. 456
JOSEPH MILNER

Even some agnostics and atheists acknowledge the moral relevance of Scriptures to society. However, the Bible gives morality a secondary place under doctrine; just like icing on a cake. How many want to eat icing for icing's sake?

...Learning and philosophy, unless duly subordinate to the revealed Will of God are no friends to Christian simplicity

---

The History of the Church: Vol. I, Century Four, Chapter IV, p. 538
JOSEPH MILNER

Illiteracy is no virtue but doesn't necessarily equate to ignorance. Learning on the other hand is a good thing. However, it has a way of puffing up a man. Humility generally decreases as learning increases, especially when there are no counterbalancing virtues to check this trend.

That grace is strong indeed which melts not under the beams of prosperity

---

The History of the Church: Vol. II, Century Four, Chapter XVI, p. 35
JOSEPH MILNER

Although prosperity is a gift from God, it can be abused when taken out of bounds. Then, it becomes a source of temptation and destruction. Blessed is the man to whom God gives the grace to match his prosperity; and who exercises that grace.

Mankind are naturally more favourable to gifts than graces
and even good men are but too ready to suppose there is much of the latter
wherever there appears an abundance of the former

The History of the Church: Vol. II, Century Four, Chapter XXIV, p. 96
JOSEPH MILNER

A man's gifts are usually more obvious than his graces. Here lies the paradox. Seldom do people have gifts and graces in equal proportion. Men with abundant gifts often have little graces; and are prone to drift into self-delusion and hypocrisy. Similarly, those with abundant graces often have little gifts; and as such, are usually relegated to the background. However, these relegated gems are often the silent pillars upholding a congregation through hidden labours of prayer and fasting. This is a lesson and warning to believers and their spiritual leaders.

...to live in the world and yet remain separate from it
shows a divine strength indeed

The History of the Church: Vol. II, Century Five, Chapter X, p. 261
JOSEPH MILNER

Aren't there many believers today whose separation from the world are superficial because their hearts are so entangled with it? Some church goers are no different from moral unbelievers because they lack holiness of heart. After all, the heart (mind) is source of our motives and actions.

False religion, in all ages, hates the light
and supports herself by persecution, not by instruction

The History of the Church: Vol. II, Century Nine, Chapter II, p. 495
JOSEPH MILNER

A creed which needs to be forced on people has no relationship with truth. Truth is the strongest notion ever. Why does it need the crutch of force to stand straight before sincere seekers?

A true Christian is a scarce bird in the world

The History of the Church: Vol. V, Century Sixteen, Chapter XI, p. 218
JOSEPH MILNER

This is the plain truth. All this swelling number of professing Christians is just a mirage. Is it any wonder the hardness of convincing church goers, through Scriptures, of the importance of high and holy living?

So little dependence is to be placed on councils
and so necessary is the aid of the Holy Spirit
that men may adhere steadfastly to the Word of God

The History of the Church: Vol. V, Century Sixteen, Chapter XIV, p. 465
JOSEPH MILNER

One of Vance Havner's sarcasms comes to mind, and I paraphrase: "...have you ever heard of a revival happening in a committee meeting?" Committees have their proper place. They shouldn't be neglected nor should they be enthroned.

K

Ken Blanchard & Norman Vincent Peale
Khalil Gibran

Ken Blanchard & Norman Vincent Peale

People with humility don't think less of themselves
they just think of themselves less

The Power of Ethical Management
KEN BLANCHARD & NORMAN VINCENT PEALE

Humility involves placing oneself in proper perspective relative to others. It doesn't mean self-destruction or self-neglect. There are many who practise some of these things but are as proud as can be. C. S. Lewis in "The Screwtape Letters" speaks of that man as taking "...pride at his own humility..." What a dangerous place to be!

Khalil Gibran

He who wears his morality but as his best garment were better naked

The Prophet
KHALIL GIBRAN

Your daily life is your temple and your religion

The Prophet
KHALIL GIBRAN

A man's morality must be his everyday clothes; else, he quickly becomes a hypocrite. A religion which cannot withstand everyday practice is a delusion. What good is a seasonal morality in a world of everyday evil?

Verily the kindness that gazes upon itself in a mirror turns to stone
And a good deed that calls itself by tender names
becomes the parent to a curse

The Prophet
KHALIL GIBRAN

Men who do benevolent deeds for men's praise already have their rewards. They will receive none in the next life. Even in this life, people will eventually perceive the shallow and wicked motives behind their deeds. We are yet to fully discover the extent of self-service this world has suffered from the hands of many so-called "philanthropists."

L

Leonard Ravenhill

Leonard Ravenhill

No man is greater than his prayer life
The pastor who is not praying is playing
The people who are not praying are straying

Why Revival Tarries, p. 25
LEONARD RAVENHILL

We sing, "Prayer is the key, prayer is the key, prayer is the master key..." However, do we ever pause to ponder those words? How deficient are you in prayer?

The secret of praying is praying in secret

Why Revival Tarries, p. 26
LEONARD RAVENHILL

What a word! Those who are dutifully attend public prayer to the neglect of private prayer are joking. If at all there ought to be a scale of preference, private devotion should come before public worship. As much as leaders ought to encourage corporate fellowship, they must ensure that God's people are earnestly seeking Him in their closets.

...but to be much for God, we must be much with God

Why Revival Tarries, p. 26
LEONARD RAVENHILL

How can you represent someone you're unfamiliar with? Can you be Christ's ambassador by hearing much about Him but knowing little of Him? The Bible is a proper starting point.

M

Mack Tomlinson

...if some pastors preached what the Lord wanted them to
some would be fired

In Light of Eternity: The Life of Leonard Ravenhill, Chapter 12, p. 200
MACK M. TOMLINSON

It is pitiful to see spiritual leaders gambling with their congregants. They preach sermons that tickle men's ears rather than burn their hearts unto repentance and holy living. Is it then surprising to find so much evil in the Church and increasing rottenness in our society today? May it not be that God has already fired many pastors while allowing them to be figureheads on the pulpit? Popular acceptance among men is no conclusive stamp of God's approval.

You'll be offered things by some people. You must shun them all...
Don't let anything come into your life
to take the Word of God out of your mouth

In Light of Eternity: The Life of Leonard Ravenhill, Chapter 13, p. 229
MACK M. TOMLINSON

Watch out for those gifts, favours and honours which wicked men use to buy people's consciences. Stand for truth: it is worth more than all the riches of this world.

A godly man can do more for your life in three days
than someone with a mixed message can do in thirty years

In Light of Eternity: The Life of Leonard Ravenhill, Chapter 13, p. 229
MACK M. TOMLINSON

Unfortunately, many spiritual leaders are such smooth operators. They have invented ways to rationalize their betrayal of divine trust. How many spiritual leaders today can you perceive to be godly men? How many of them do you draw close to? We naturally don't like associating with those whose lifestyles reveal the shallowness of ours.

Our pulpits have more puppets than prophets

In Light of Eternity: The Life of Leonard Ravenhill, Chapter 16, p. 280
Mack M. Tomlinson

Not only that, some of these "pulpiteers" are smoother than politicians. The difference is that they use the Bible as a cloak for their treachery. How many preachers are bold enough to denounce evil today?

We have politicians, but no statesman, preachers but no prophets

In Light of Eternity: The Life of Leonard Ravenhill, Chapter 16, p. 285
Mack M. Tomlinson

Historically, today isn't much different. There are many authority-figures who sell their principles to appease the people, and invent ways of silencing true leaders.

Form in preaching is a terribly small matter...
Conviction of sin and divine empowering are the great issues in preaching

In Light of Eternity: The Life of Leonard Ravenhill, Chapter 17, p. 329
Mack M. Tomlinson

... every preacher needs to be reminded that
he is not a descendant of the Greek orator
but is the offspring of the Hebrew prophet

In Light of Eternity: The Life of Leonard Ravenhill, Chapter 18, p. 340
Mack M. Tomlinson

When focus on our calling is lost, we quickly accumulate props to simulate its appearance. It's high time we left irrelevancies and refocused on the main issue; sin as man's greatest problem and his needs of the Saviour. A preacher ought not to be too picky about the means to this end, so long as it isn't sinful.

… [never] embrace tradition at the expense of the truth

In Light of Eternity: The Life of Leonard Ravenhill, Chapter 19, p. 384
MACK M. TOMLINSON

Naturally, we value traditions as human beings. They give us a sense of unity, direction and purpose. However, ungodly traditions can quickly become entrenched in a group. If that happens, how would you respond to those traditions which are anti-truth?

The man who will not lay down his lifestyle for God
will never lay down his life for [Him]

In Light of Eternity: The Life of Leonard Ravenhill, Chapter 22, p. 430
MACK M. TOMLINSON

Now I'm not talking about legalism or denominational traditions. I'm talking about things which unbelievers practice and know that a believer shouldn't. One of these is worldly dressing. Today, many so-called preachers, pastors and spiritual leaders support these questionable lifestyles. Obviously, some of them are smart enough to produce extra-biblical arguments. However, some dogmatically produce contorted and deformed arguments from the Bible. I said all that to tell you this: be very deliberate in evaluating any doctrine under the Light of Scriptures. As they say, "There are many who would take Jesus Christ as their Saviour but never as their Lord."

Madame de Stael

The voice of conscience is so delicate that it is easy to stifle it
but it is also so clear that it is impossible to mistake it

MADAME DE STAEL

If you don't believe that conscience exits, you have probably stifled yours over the years. Similarly, a man can so lie to himself repeatedly that he eventually believes the lie to be true.

Mahatma Ghandi

Seven deadly sins:
Wealth without Work
Pleasure without Conscience
Science without Humanity
Knowledge without Character
Politics without Principle
Commerce without Morality
Worship without Sacrifice

MAHATMA GHANDI

There are limits, rules and borders in life. Man isn't meant to live like beasts. Examine yourself in light of this list.

Malcolm Gladwell

Achievement is talent plus preparation

Outliers, p. 38
MALCOLM GLADWELL

Practice isn't the thing you do once you're good
It's the thing you do that makes you good

Outliers, p. 42
MALCOLM GLADWELL

As John Maxwell said, "Talent is never enough." Preparation is the crux of the matter. It ought to be a lifestyle for sustainable achievement.

Those three things —
autonomy, complexity, and a connection between effort and reward
— are, most people agree
the three qualities that work has to have if it is to be satisfying

Outliers, p. 149
MALCOLM GLADWELL

Hard work is a prison sentence only if it does not have meaning

Outliers, p. 150
MALCOLM GLADWELL

Work becomes fun while doing what you love and loving what you do. How many lead "lives of quiet desperation" today as Henry Thoreau puts it, due to this missing link?

Matthew Henry

God consults our benefit rather than our desires
for He knows what is good for us better than we do for ourselves
and how long it is fit our restraints to continue and desired mercies delayed

Bible Commentary, Gen. 8:13-14
MATTHEW HENRY

Little wonder that we only understand in hindsight how God's denial or delayed response to prayers was best for us. In the heat of the moment, desire makes us dumb and numb to the whole picture.

Drunken porters keep open gates

Bible Commentary, Gen. 9:18-23
MATTHEW HENRY

This is true in the physical and spiritual senses. Leaders, parents, mentors and the likes are porters. When drunk with the wine of lies or hypocrisy, they stand at the gate alright but see nothing enter or leave. Wouldn't it be better for people to have open gates than drunken porters as guards?

Poverty and travail, wants and wanderings
could not separate between Abram and Lot
but riches did

Bible Commentary, Gen. 13:5-9
MATTHEW HENRY

Quite an interesting observation. Riches aren't always a blessing. They could quickly become our worst nightmare.

Though civility teaches us to call others by their highest titles
yet humility and wisdom teaches us to call ourselves by the lowest

Bible Commentary, Gen. 16:7-9
Matthew Henry

This tenuous balance between civility and humility ought to be the hallmark of Christian relationships.

Note, children and servants must be treated with mildness and gentleness
lest we provoke them to take any irregular courses
and so become accessory to their sins
which will condemn us though it will not justify them

Bible Commentary, Gen. 16:7-9
Matthew Henry

We ought to be very careful how we treat others: wards, dependants, subordinates, mentees and so on. This is not just a lesson in politeness or civility but an evidence of practical holiness. You can claim to be white as snow internally yet crimson-stained by your evil attitude towards others.

It is an easier thing to persuade men to assume the form of godliness
than to submit to the power of godliness

Bible Commentary, Gen. 16:15-16
Matthew Henry

Hypocrisy is a natural propensity common to man. We need a power greater than us to keep it in check.

God's favourites are often the world's laughingstocks

Bible Commentary, Gen. 21:1-8
Matthew Henry

You aren't alone. Don't feel forsaken and isolated when you experience this. Although it's easier said then done, consider it a badge of honour and sign of divine approval.

We must not, under the colour of shunning bad company
be sour of all company, and jealous of everybody

Bible Commentary, Gen. 21:22-32
Matthew Henry

Seclusion and contentiousness aren't marks of holiness. Holiness ought to make you peaceable, even with foes, as much as lies in your power.

Note, where we have a tent God must have an Altar
where we have a house He must have a Church in it

Bible Commentary, Gen. 33:16-20
Matthew Henry

As an individual, when last did you offer sacrifices of praise, worship and prayer to God where you live? As a married person, when last did you pray with your spouse, children and other members of your household?

It is a common thing, but a very bad thing
to cover malice against men's persons with a show of zeal against their vices

Bible Commentary, Gen. 38:24-30
Matthew Henry

Hypocrisy is such a slippery slope into which many inadvertently veer and on which many purposefully chose to slide.

Constancy is a virtue, but obstinacy is not

Bible Commentary, Gen. 43:11-14
Matthew Henry

It isn't right to remain adamant when change is clearly the best and principled option.

Present satisfactions should not take us off
from the consideration and prospect of future inconveniences
which possibly may arise from what now appears most promising

Bible Commentary, Gen. 46:1-4
Matthew Henry

The best course of action today might not be the most appealing. Although this distinction can only be made after careful consideration, it requires courage and determination to make the right choice.

Modesty is a great ornament to dignity

Bible Commentary, Gen. 50:1-6
MATTHEW HENRY

Men are usually proud of the dignity conferred on them. However, true modesty keeps men of dignity humble. It adds gracious sweetness to their dignity.

Even good men are apt to cool in their zeal for God and duty
when they have long been deprived of the society of the faithful
Solitude has its advantages
but they seldom counterbalance the loss of Christian communion

Bible Commentary, Ex. 4:24-31
MATTHEW HENRY

This society of the faithful could be gotten through books and audio-visual recordings. If and when situation permits however, Christian communion ought to be face-to-face and not virtual.

Those that are called out to public service for God and their generation
must expect to be tried, not only by the malicious threats of proud enemies
but by the unjust and unkind censures of unthinking friends
who judge only by outward appearance
and look but a little way before them

Bible Commentary, Ex. 5:15-23
MATTHEW HENRY

Any man who puts himself in public position must be ready to endure just and unjust scrutiny. As Vance Havner once said and I paraphrase: that man needs "...to have the heart of a child, the mind of a scholar and the hide of a rhinoceros...Now the challenge is how to harden your hide without hardening your heart." We need to be considerate and compassionate when talking to or about others.

God warns before He wounds

Bible Commentary, Ex. 7:14-25
MATTHEW HENRY

God is no tyrant. He is Just, even in the discipline of His children. Some have found fault with His destruction of children and women in the Bible. However, these people forget that their judgement is limited to what is revealed in Scriptures. What about those details that are hidden from us but are ever present before the Omniscient and Omnipresent God?

Till the heart is renewed by the Grace of God
the impressions made by the force of affliction do not abide
the convictions wear off, and the promises that were extorted are forgotten
Till the disposition of the air changes
what thaws in the sun will freeze again in the shade

Bible Commentary, Ex. 8:1-15
MATTHEW HENRY

Morality isn't necessarily holiness. A moral man's heart might still be obsessed with dark motives and filthy goals. However, a holy man's heart is driven by heavenly passions. Salvation which brings heart transformation isn't gotten by works. It's a grace imparted through faith. Until then, the power to work out and maintain this gift of Salvation is unavailable.

However God in His providence is pleased to advance us
we must make conscience of giving honour to whom honour is due
and never look with disdain upon our poor relations
Those that stand high in the favour of God
are not thereby discharged from the duty they owe to men
nor will that justify them in a stately haughty carriage

Bible Commentary, Ex. 18:7-12
MATTHEW HENRY

Religion does not destroy good manners

Bible Commentary, Ex. 18:7-12
MATTHEW HENRY

Wisdom and humility aren't meant just for those in lowly positions, nor are they solely for the unbeliever or irreligious. Religion shouldn't be used as a cloak for wickedness.

There may be over-doing even in well-doing
and therefore our zeal must always be governed by discretion
that our good may not be evil spoken of

Bible Commentary, Ex. 18:13-27
MATTHEW HENRY

Just because something is right doesn't justify obnoxiousness in its execution. Even right must be circumscribed by wisdom and humility.

Advice must be given
with a humble submission to the Word and Providence of God
which must always overrule

Bible Commentary, Ex. 18:13-27
MATTHEW HENRY

This is a warning to spiritual counsellors, leaders and mentors. It's a slippery slope to device Scripture-based formulas and forget or refuse to subject them to the approval of the God of the Scriptures.

Those are not so wise as they would be thought to be
who think themselves too wise to be counseled
for a wise man (one who is truly so) will hear, and will increase learning
and not slight good counsel though given by an inferior

Bible Commentary, Ex. 18:13-27
MATTHEW HENRY

Humility before all men is one hallmark of a wise man. It is an avenue through which a man increases and improves his wisdom.

Pride makes a god of self
covetousness makes a god of money
sensuality makes a god of the belly
whatever is esteemed or loved, feared or served, delighted in or depended on more than God
that (whatever it is) we do in effect make a god of

Bible Commentary, Ex. 20:1-11
MATTHEW HENRY

This explains idolatry in practical language. It goes beyond bowing before molten or graven images.

A man may ruin himself through mere carelessness
but he cannot save himself without great care and circumspection

Bible Commentary, Ex. 23:10-19
MATTHEW HENRY

Christian love or liberality doesn't mean carelessness: the propensity to accept everyone's conviction as right. Love can quickly be distorted into indulgence if it isn't circumscribed by counterbalancing virtues.

Note, those whose office it is to instruct
must do it by example as well as precept

Bible Commentary, Lev. 21:1-9
MATTHEW HENRY

Teachers and leaders must watch their lives as well as their message. They must ensure that both are consistent.

The way to preserve the peace of the Church is to preserve the purity of it

Bible Commentary, Lev. 24:10-23
MATTHEW HENRY

Don't limit the word "peace" to lack of physical and emotional distress. Extend it to the spiritual and eternal dimensions.

And sometimes
the unkindness of our friends is a greater trial of our meekness
than the malice of our enemies

Bible Commentary, Num. 12:1-3
MATTHEW HENRY

It is easier to overlook the wrongs from enemies due to their ignorance or evil intentions. However, it is hard to excuse the unkindness of friends who ought to know better. This is where God's Grace shines in a life.

...great dignity exposes us to great iniquity

Bible Commentary, Num. 18:1-7
MATTHEW HENRY

This is one reason humility is a counterbalancing virtue that ought to accompany dignity.

A man may be full of the knowledge of God
and yet utterly destitute of the Grace of God
may receive the truth in the light of it
and yet be a stranger to the love of it

Bible Commentary, Num. 24:15-25
MATTHEW HENRY

A man might give his back and hands to a cause while his heart is far way. Hypocrisy comes in different shades, and makes it easy for a careless man to fool himself.

Religion must never be made a cloak for injustice

Bible Commentary, Deut. 2:1-7
MATTHEW HENRY

It is a very terrible thing to perpetrate evil in the name or under the guise of religion. Of all consequences, that man blocks others on the road of religion or who are considering it.

The comfortable cheerful using of what God has given us
with temperance and sobriety
is really the honouring of God with it

Bible Commentary, Deut. 14:22-29
MATTHEW HENRY

Remember that sadness and moroseness are not synonymous with holiness. However, joy that is acceptable before God must be circumscribed by the twin pillars of temperance and sobriety.

Modesty is the hedge of chastity
and therefore ought to be very carefully preserved and kept up by both sexes

Bible Commentary, Deut. 25:5-12
MATTHEW HENRY

The doctrine that God only looks or is more interested in the heart and not the body isn't biblical. It's a loophole meant to slide men en masse into perdition. If chastity is purely a matter of the heart, when did the heart stop being affected by the senses and vice versa? Mull that one over. Although modesty seems closer to the external domain, it is still one manifestation of a man's internal condition.

Those that are bound for heaven must be willing to swim against the stream
and must not do as the most do but as the best do

Bible Commentary, Josh. 24:15-28
MATTHEW HENRY

This heaven-bound journey is no mere walk in the park. Willingness to swim against the stream of culture, traditions and society is one thing; actually doing it and how it's done are other things. Willingness doesn't often produce action; and "the means always determines the end."

Many are melted under the Word
that harden again before they are cast into a new mould

Bible Commentary, Judg. 2:1-5
MATTHEW HENRY

Conviction without consecration yields little or no transformation of life. Feelings that are not backed by the will often end up as fancies. Jesus Christ spoke of new birth and being born again. Salvation ought to survive the heat of that original moment. Metaphorically speaking, that "spiritual pregnancy" could be lost due to several "spiritual accidents."

Many are led into false ways by one false step of a good man

Bible Commentary, Judg. 8:22-28
MATTHEW HENRY

This is a warning to both leaders and followers. As a leader, you ought to watch your steps because there are many closely treading your path. As a follower, carefully "look before you leap."

Honesty will be found the best policy

Bible Commentary, Ruth 4:1-8
Matthew Henry

I just thought it wise to provide one of the earliest references to several variants of this quote. This quote is still relevant today.

Parents cannot give grace to their children, nor does it run in the blood

Bible Commentary, 1 Sam. 2:11-26
Matthew Henry

Don't assess anyone on the sole basis of their family tree. After all, there are unholy people with holy parents and holy people with unholy parents. Holiness isn't hereditary.

A good cause often suffers for the sake of the bad men that undertake it

Bible Commentary, 1 Sam. 4:10-11
Matthew Henry

Be very careful who you enter into partnership with: be it marriage, business or some other venture. Generally, it is easier for evil to corrupt good than for good to purge evil.

It is much cheaper to learn by other people's experience than by our own

Bible Commentary, 1 Sam. 6:1-9
Matthew Henry

These are words of wisdom that can save a man wasted years and avoidable regrets. Do the economics and decide.

We were all ruined by an ambition of forbidden knowledge

Bible Commentary, 1 Sam. 6:19-21
Matthew Henry

As they say, "Curiosity killed the cat." May it not be that the cat isn't the only culprit here.

A friend in need is a friend indeed

Bible Commentary, 1 Sam. 19:1-7
MATTHEW HENRY

This is one of the earliest documented references of this popular saying. Your true friends are those who stick with you through trying times.

Many have great gifts and yet no grace
prophesy in Christ's name and yet are disowned by Him

Bible Commentary, 1 Sam. 19:18-24
MATTHEW HENRY

Although possessing spiritual gifts is good, having as much grace to counterbalance the gifts is better. Much grace with little gifts would sustain a man till he gets to Heaven. Little grace with much gifts might fail a man on the same journey.

It is strange if those
that associate themselves with wicked people and grow intimate with them
come off without guilt, or grief, or both

Bible Commentary, 1 Sam. 29:1-5
MATTHEW HENRY

Be deliberate in choosing your associates and those you frequently communicate with. This can have unintended consequences.

Those might gain information by poems that would not read history

---

Bible Commentary, 2 Samuel 1:17-27
MATTHEW HENRY

Poetry and music are two of the possible ways to codify messages in sizeable chunks.

...writing, that best conservatory of knowledge

Bible Commentary, 2 Samuel 1:17-27
MATTHEW HENRY

Our memories are fickle and generally grows weak with time. Today is the right time to start keeping a journal, writing your will, and documenting important information. Don't wait until it's late.

Familiarity, even with that which is most awful, is apt to breed contempt

Bible Commentary, 2 Samuel 6:6-11
MATTHEW HENRY

Familiarity in a sense is already bad on its own. It makes men trivialize people and important things. How much more when we become familiar with evil? It deadens our conscience such that we eagerly embrace the evil which once repulsed us.

...a good intention will not justify a bad action
it will not suffice to say of that which is ill done that it was well meant

Bible Commentary, 2 Samuel 6:6-11
MATTHEW HENRY

Good intentions are alright in its place. However, it is never an excuse for wrong deeds. Many have hidden and some now do hide under the guise of good intentions, to perpetrate the grossest evil. You know, hypocrisy comes in different shades of grey.

Ministers must not think that their public performances
will excuse them from their family-worship

Bible Commentary, 2 Samuel 6:20-23
MATTHEW HENRY

Isn't this one reason why the children of many ministers later turn their backs on their father's religion? Also, couldn't this be one reason why the marriages of some ministers end up in divorce after several decades?

Those are commonly most ambitious of preferment that are least fit for it
the best qualified are the most modest and self-diffident...

Bible Commentary, 2 Samuel 15:1-6
MATTHEW HENRY

Those most ambitious for preferment are so focused on the ends that
they're most willing to use any means. Also, they are somehow more sus-
ceptible to pride. This combination makes it easier for them to hurt others
and eventually leads to their downfall.

The majority is no certain rule to judge equity by

Bible Commentary, 2 Samuel 15:7-12
MATTHEW HENRY

Often, what receives the stamp of common approval might be so far
from just. Don't be ruled by the whims of the majority. A paraphrase of
one of Vance Havner's quotes is apt here, "...be guided by your conscience
which ought to be enlightened by Scriptures..."

We must not do evil that good may come of it

Bible Commentary, 2 Samuel 17:15-21
MATTHEW HENRY

As they say, "The end does not always justify the means" and "The
means determines the ends."

Great men should take heed what they say
lest any bad use be made of it by those about them

Bible Commentary, 2 Samuel 23:8-39
MATTHEW HENRY

This is a warning to those in positions of authority and power: teachers, parents, mentors, leaders and so on. None should use his personality
or temperament as an excuse in this matter. He forewent that privilege: a
"hazard" which comes with the position.

One bad act of a good man
may be of more pernicious consequence to others
than twenty of a wicked man

Bible Commentary, 1 Kings 11:1-8
MATTHEW HENRY

The Christian life is one of extreme carefulness through watching and prayer. The bar of Christian principles is Jesus Christ. Hence, we need to keep pressing forward in Him.

Those who have dominion over men
are apt to forget God's dominion over them
and, while they demand obedience from their inferiors
to deny it to him who is the Supreme

Bible Commentary, 1 Kings 11:9-13
MATTHEW HENRY

This is a timely warning to those in authority and power, especially spiritual leaders. Pride has several ways of overtaking a careless man.

Man's extremity is God's opportunity of magnifying his own power
his time to appear for his people is when their strength is gone...

Bible Commentary, 2 Kings 7:1-2
MATTHEW HENRY

As Jason Crabb sang, "...it might look too difficult, it might look impossible, but O! God let it be, a chance for a miracle..." How can God showcase Himself while you're still drawing attention to yourself on the stage? Vance Havner once said that, God is "a Soloist not an accompanist."

Honours change men's tempers and manners, and seldom for the better...

Bible Commentary, 2 Kings 8:7-15
MATTHEW HENRY

A Christian ought to guard himself against this subtle enemy called pride.

When men choose wives for themselves
they must remember they are choosing mothers for their children
and are concerned to choose accordingly

Bible Commentary, 2 Kings 8:25-29
MATTHEW HENRY

A priceless advice to unmarried men seeking marriage. It can also be extended to unmarried women: not to accept any suitor's proposal on superficial grounds.

We are blessed in order that we may be blessings

Bible Commentary, 1 Chronicles 14:1-7
MATTHEW HENRY

God isn't in the business of raising selfish sons and daughters, but children who will truly reflect His Image.

The church's poorest times were its purest

Bible Commentary, 1 Chronicles 16:1-6
MATTHEW HENRY

Unbridled comfort and tranquillity has a way of dampening spiritual fervency.

Assisting the devotion of others will not atone for our own neglects

Bible Commentary, 2 Chronicles 8:12-18
MATTHEW HENRY

As good as volunteering for Church programmes and preparing the hearts of others through music is, they don't automatically edify the performing ministers. A man still needs to privately minister to himself through prayer, Bible study, praise and worship, fasting and other spiritual exercises. Alternatively, it could be through sitting under others to receive edification. Else, he will quickly wither from the root up.

It is easier to build temples than to be temples of God

Bible Commentary, 2 Chronicles 24:1-14
MATTHEW HENRY

Your greatest opposition is usually your self. It can come in the form of subtle and beautified hypocrisy: doing external good works at the expense of the ultimate work, which is internal.

Bibles are jewels
but, thanks be to God, they are not rarities

Bible Commentary, 2 Chronicles 34:14-28
Matthew Henry

What a privilege to live in a time when many have access to the Bible in several formats, translations and languages.

If every one will sweep before his own door
the street will be clean...

Bible Commentary, Nehemiah 3:1-32
Matthew Henry

Christian, carefully watch over your life and the purity of the Church will be preserved by God's Grace. Don't go around causing offences among the brethren while claiming unintentionality and a pure heart. In another quote, Matthew Henry responds to such people like this, "...it will not suffice to say of that which is ill done that it was well meant."

If we think to secure ourselves by prayer only, without watchfulness
we are slothful and tempt God
if by watchfulness, without prayer
we are proud and slight God
and, either way, we forfeit his protection

Bible Commentary, Nehemiah 4:7-15
Matthew Henry

Don't expect God to do what He has given you power to do.

Note, Reproofs must be given with great consideration
that what is well meant may not come short of its end
for want of being well managed
It is the reproof of instruction that giveth life

Bible Commentary, Nehemiah 5:6-13
Matthew Henry

This is a timely word of caution to every Christian. Often, it is the wrong means that mars the intended good end.

Note, Even nobles and rulers, if they do that which is evil ought to be told of it by proper persons

Bible Commentary, Nehemiah 5:6-13
MATTHEW HENRY

This is applicable to the Church today. Consider how Apostle Paul openly confronted Apostle Peter in Galatians 2:1-14. Notice how he was in the right position to do so: as a fellow Apostle and as the Apostle to the Gentiles. There might have been others who noticed the fault in Apostle Peter's behaviour, but weren't in the right position of authority to address it. Disaster is nearby when a leader has no one who can put him in check.

Nothing exposes religion more to the reproach of its enemies than the worldliness and hard-heartedness of the professors of it

Bible Commentary, Nehemiah 5:6-13
MATTHEW HENRY

Dear Christian, is there worldliness and hard-heartedness in your life?

. . . for dead walls, without living watchmen are but a poor defence to a city

Bible Commentary, Nehemiah 7:1-4
MATTHEW HENRY

By extension, a church without true prophets or which silences her prophets is headed for judgement.

Those that fear God must evidence it by their being faithful to all men and universally conscientious

Bible Commentary, Nehemiah 7:1-4
MATTHEW HENRY

Conscientiousness appears to be a forgotten virtue, even in today's church. Many use their natural temperaments to excuse their failure in this area. Dr. Henry Brandt in Tim Lahaye's "I Love You, But Why Are We So Different" gave a beautiful response to this group of people. He said, "You can use your background as an excuse for present behaviour only until you become a Christian. After that it is no longer a valid excuse." I completely agree with him on the basis of 2 Corinthians 5:17, which says, "Therefore if any man be in Christ, he is a new creature: old things are passed away; behold, all things are become new."

Whom God intends to honour he first humbles and lays low...

Bible Commentary, Job 4:12-21
Matthew Henry

This fine thread runs throughout Scriptures. Consider Abraham, Joseph, Moses, Elijah, Daniel and his three friends and Paul; just to name a few.

Sanctified civility is a great ornament to Christianity

The Life of Philip Henry, p. 11
Matthew Henry (J. B. Williams, ed.)

Christianity doesn't sanction rudeness or moroseness. If you can't follow peace with your fellow man (irrespective of his beliefs or status), how can you claim to be a Christian, i.e. Christ-like?

...for grace doth not run in the blood
...even godly parents have wicked children

The Life of Philip Henry, p. 31
Matthew Henry (J. B. Williams, ed.)

Don't judge a man's character or beliefs (good or bad) solely on the basis of his parents'. In essence, a man isn't predestined in the practical sense, by his family tree.

...those who would have comfort in that change of their condition
must see to it that they bring none of the guilt of the sins of their single state
into the married state

The Life of Philip Henry, p. 42
Matthew Henry (J. B. Williams, ed.)

This is a warning and advice to unmarried folks seeking marriage. Do yourself and your future spouse a favour by getting your life in order now. Deal decisively with every besetting sin, bad addictions and bad traits before trapping someone else into your vortex.

Let prayer be the key of the morning, and the bolt of the night

---

The Life of Philip Henry, p. 45
MATTHEW HENRY (J. B. WILLIAMS, ED.)

This is a sound counsel for facing life's battles. Prayer will keep your conscious mind anchored on the Lord during the day and give your subconscious mind food for meditation through the night.

...the best picture of a minister is in the hearts of his people

---

The Life of Philip Henry, p. 127
MATTHEW HENRY (J. B. WILLIAMS, ED.)

A minister's duty isn't primarily to acquire degrees, complete "spiritual" projects and organize focus groups. If all these are ends in themselves and not tools to positively impact his congregants and others, that minister isn't worth his salt.

...thanks-giving is good, but thanks-living is better

The Life of Philip Henry, p. 127
MATTHEW HENRY (J. B. WILLIAMS, ED.)

Do people give thanks to God for their paths having crossed yours in life? Many professors of Christianity are "sound as a dot in their doctrine," as Vance Havner would say, and yet live such unbecoming lives.

God must have the flower of our age
The beloved disciple was the youngest of the disciples

The Life of Philip Henry, p. 185
MATTHEW HENRY (J. B. WILLIAMS, ED.)

The beloved disciple here refers to John the Apostle, the brother of James and the son of Zebedee. No man is too young to dedicate his best to God. Don't wait till old age; you might not live that long. If you do, your physical strength might not match your will.

It is said that fishes first putrefy in the head; — so do many

The Life of Philip Henry, p. 202
Matthew Henry (J. B. Williams, ed.)

Watch the thoughts you entertain. Wrong thinking is a terrible disease that will affect the entire man. Properly weigh ideas and prophecies against the Scriptures. This guards you against falsehood. Faulty theology is a slippery slope which quickly descends to outright heresy.

It is a rare sight to see old people melt in tears for sin

The Life of Philip Henry, p. 205
Matthew Henry (J. B. Williams, ed.)

This is still applicable today. It is true that age brings a certain level of wisdom and maturity. However, none is infallible. The rarity of this brokenness in older folks could be a pointer to their loss or lack of humility and spiritual sensitivity. Of course, I don't mean all of them.

Maya Angelou

The historically oppressed can find not only sanctity
but safety in the state of victimization

Singin' and Swingin' and Gettin' Merry Like Christmas, p. 75
Maya Angelou

There are many who prefer the status quo, no matter how unpleasant, because of its benefits. They are willing to cling to the security they've known than to risk it for an uncertain liberty.

Preparation is rarely easy and never beautiful

Singin' and Swingin' and Gettin' Merry Like Christmas, p. 133
Maya Angelou

However, the end product is usually worth the whole pain.

Avarice cripples virtue and lies in ambush for honesty

Singin' and Swingin' and Gettin' Merry Like Christmas, p. 205
Maya Angelou

According to 1 Timothy 6:6, "But godliness with contentment is great gain." This is one of the best defences against avarice.

Michael Gerber

When the dream is gone, the only thing left is work
The tyranny of routine

The e-Myth Revisited
MICHAEL GERBER

Dream as used here could be understood as vision and not necessarily sleepy-dream. Any who loses sight of the vision during the mission ends up working for work's sake. None is above slipping into this routine if the vision (end goal) isn't always kept in view.

People have the unerring ability
to forget everything they start and to be distracted by trivia

---

The e-Myth Revisited
MICHAEL GERBER

Never lose focus on your. Be deliberate about how you invest your time, energy and resources. Drop every side project which can detour you from reaching your goal(s).

... which is not to say that we don't care about anything
we obviously do...
But I think that the things we have come to care about
are insignificant when placed on the scale...

The e-Myth Revisited
MICHAEL GERBER

Mere activity will not produce any significant results; productive activity could. The first step is identifying which of these productive activities promise the most futuristic significance or will contribute most to it. These should be your focus from now on.

The problem is. . . we're just not very serious people these days
We even speak about values. . . as though they are a commodity
like a sweater or a pair of Gucci pumps
that can be acquired by writing a check

The e-Myth Revisited
Michael Gerber

Paying lip service is as bad as outright lying. Values are not goods and services to be bought by the highest bidder. Only unserious people consider them as such. Values are acquired through long and strenuous discipline.

When you hear something, you will forget it
When you see something, you will remember it
But not until you do something, will you understand it

The e-Myth Revisited
Michael Gerber

This is another way of saying, "Practice makes perfect." The more you do something, the less you know about that thing, and the more you know that thing.

Mike Mason

In one way or another, religion may be used not to glorify God at all
but actually to shift the emphasis from God to man
and to do so in a way that drips with piety

The Mystery of Marriage, p. 40
MIKE MASON

Quite a way to put it. You know, hypocrisy can be so beautiful on the outside.

The Lord God made woman out of part of man's side
and closed up the place with flesh
but in marriage He reopens this empty, aching place in man
and begins the process of putting the woman back again
if not literally in the side, then certainly at it
permanently there, intrusively there
a sudden lifelong resident of a space which until that point
the man will have considered to be his own private territory, his own body

The Mystery of Marriage, p. 47
MIKE MASON

Marriage is beautiful but involves some inconveniences that are requisite for growth.

Monica Mendez Leahy

Your marriage is about your average day, not your wedding day

1001 Questions To Ask Before You Get Married, p. 93
MONICA MENDEZ LEAHY

A wedding is one day, your marriage is for the rest of your life

1001 Questions To Ask Before You Get Married, p. 94
MONICA MENDEZ LEAHY

Many get this mixed up. They spend their life-savings and emotional resources on the wedding with little preparation on making their marriage survive the journey.

O

O. J. Kuye
Orison Swett Marden

O. J. Kuye

Passion without discipline produce derelicts

Born To Be Great, p. 158
O. J. KUYE

Boundaries exist in life for a reason. All this doctrine of being oneself and doing one's thing is only reasonable when circumscribed by principles.

Being busy does not always mean real work

Born To Overcome, p. 79
THOMAS EDISON
IN O. J. KUYE

Be very particular how you spend your time. Don't waste your resources on trivia. Take time to evaluate your pursuits in light of this.

Orison Swett Marden

The way always opens for the determined soul, the man of faith and courage

ORISON SWETT MARDEN

Persistence will eventually wear out or at least weaken the strongest resistance. Keep at it.

P

Philip Yancey
Piet Hein
Plutarch

Philip Yancey

...attempts to compel morality tend to produce
defiant subjects and tyrannical rulers who lose their moral core

The Jesus I Never Knew, p. 75-76
PHILIP YANCEY

Good intentions are insufficient reasons for doing something. This is applicable even in the family: between parents and children, among siblings, and so on. After all, "The means determines the end" and "The end does not always justify the means."

God's terrible insistence on human freedom is so absolute
that he granted us the power to live as though he did not exist
to spit in his face, to crucify him

The Jesus I Never Knew, p. 78
PHILIP YANCEY

As much as this is true, never forget the coming Day of Judgement. Then, God will sit as the Just Judge to evaluate how we've used this precious freedom.

...the excitement generated by miracles
did not readily convert into life-changing faith...
Although faith may produce miracles, miracles do not necessarily produce faith

The Jesus I Never Knew, p. 166, 170
PHILIP YANCEY

Faith and miracles aren't necessarily mutually exclusive. However, it is easier to go from faith to miracles than from miracles to faith.

History shows that when the church uses the tools of the world's kingdom it becomes as ineffectual, or as tyrannical, as any other power structure

---

The Jesus I Never Knew, p. 246
Philip Yancey

"The means doesn't always justify the end," no matter the nobility of that end. This is also applicable to personal interactions.

Piet Hein

Problems worthy of attack prove their worth by hitting back

Piet Hein

Don't expect an easy ride when dealing with a problem worth its salt. Brace yourself for the storm.

Plutarch

The mind is not a vessel to be filled
but a fire to be ignited

PLUTARCH

Truly, the mind is a vessel. Simply filling it isn't enough. It ought to be vigorously applied and exercise aright.

R

Richard Wurmbrand
Robert Collier
Robert Kiyosaki
Roberts Liardon
Ronald Coase
Russell Conwell

Richard Wurmbrand

Christian books are like good wine, the older the better

In God's Underground, p. 50
RICHARD WURMBRAND

What a succinct way to put it! Our technological advancements haven't made the Bible obsolete. In fact, the closer you move to the present, the shallower the theology of many so-called Christian books. Agreed, we have more fanfare and pretty buildings today as places of worship. However, many Christian best-sellers are so feel-goody that you could mistake the author's primary calling as motivational speaking instead of biblical preaching.

When the mouth is too much open, even to speak good
the soul loses its fire just as a room loses warmth through an open door

In God's Underground, p. 50
RICHARD WURMBRAND

Talkativeness in any form is often a vice. As they say, "God gave us two ears and one mouth for a reason." Think this one over.

Robert Collier

In all nature, to cease to grow is to perish

The Secret of the Ages
ROBERT COLLIER

Man was created for a purpose-driven life. His choice of purpose and the means to pursue it could be evil or good. Nevertheless, the pursuit of a definite purpose provides him with the drive that fuels his sense of fulfilment and wellbeing. As they say, "growth is a key characteristic of living things." Let's consider growth in the positive sense. Once an institution, family or group stops investing in themselves positively, others who do will overtake them. Hence, a refusal to grow is an approval to die; even it happens at a gradual rate. That person or group eventually becomes all shoot with no root; alive outside but dead inside. Therefore, find your purpose for living and pursue it wholeheartedly.

Luck or fortune is a fickle jade
that smiles most often on those who need her least

The Secret of the Ages
ROBERT COLLIER

Have you ever noticed that those who have a reasonable amount of resources seem to attract more? This holds true, even after discounting those who get their fortune through ill means. One common denominator is the willingness to step out and try, over and over again. They don't just sit around waiting for opportunities to knock on their doors. Instead, they go out searching in the highways and byways. What are you waiting for? Today is your best day to step out in faith.

You've got to get up every morning with determination
if you're going to go to bed that night with satisfaction

The Secret of the Ages
ROBERT COLLIER

Man was made to live a productive life. His sense of wellness and wholeness is tied to achieving something. Hence, a sense of emptiness haunts a man with no passionate desire for achieving his goals. What you can't view afar by morning can't be closer by night. See everyday as a new chance to get it right.

One of the signs of a really big man, you know,
is his eagerness to learn from everyone and anything

The Secret of the Ages
ROBERT COLLIER

Never grow too big to the point of overestimating your strengths, underestimating your weaknesses and looking for new ways to educate everyone else. This is a slope so slippery, that it can take anyone by surprise.

You are only as old as your mind

The Secret of the Ages
ROBERT COLLIER

God gave us a mind as creative as it can get. It is better if a man's body can't keep up with his mind due to things like physical age, than vice versa. What you often meditate upon becomes your reality. Watch what you feed your mind. Don't expose yourself to sounds, sights and situations you don't want replicated and multiplied in your life. Exercise the muscles of your mind with the right materials.

Robert Kiyosaki

Security and Freedom are not the same...in fact they are opposites
The more security you seek the less freedom you have
The people with the most security are in jail

Before You Quit Your Job
ROBERT KIYOSAKI

The more a person seeks security
the more that person gives up control over their life

Retire Young Retire Rich
ROBERT KIYOSAKI

There has been a push for more governmental involvement in the affairs of citizens. This will bring more security alright; but at the cost of individual freedom. Many of us forget that the demand for more rights ought to go with more responsibilities. If you demand more rights but are unwilling to take up the counterbalancing responsibilities, you will have to pay someone else to take up the slack. This payment often comes in the form of the loss of certain freedoms or rights.

In times of change...Learners inherit the earth
while the learned find themselves beautifully equipped
to deal with a world that no longer exists

Cashflow Quadrant
ERIK HOFFER
IN ROBERT KIYOSAKI

Keep your knowledge up to date. Ensure that your current skill set always exceeds the maximum requirements of your occupation or business.

I never let schooling interfere with my education

Cashflow Quadrant
MARK TWAIN
IN ROBERT KIYOSAKI

Going to school is one thing. Getting an education is another thing. You can get education inside or outside a school. School attendance doesn't automatically translate to education. After all, there are many schooled people with little education and many unschooled people with much education. It is all a matter of mind exposure and not just physical attendance. Schooling has a completion date but education has none. Keep up your education. Read great books. Listen to useful audio-visual recordings. Attend life-transforming seminars.

It is okay to be five years early, but not one day late

Retire Young Retire Rich
ROBERT KIYOSAKI

If you arrive early, the worst thing will be to patiently wait. If you arrive late, the best thing will be to partake of what is left. Think that one over. Nowadays, people see lateness as one of their personality traits instead of a character flaw. If a man can't stick to time, would you like him to represent you? Punctuality is a virtue and not just a personality trait. Start working on it.

Roberts Liardon

...I have set up for myself the rule that
whenever I discern a sounder opinion in any matter whatsoever
I gladly and humbly abandon the earlier one
For I know that those things I have learned are
but the least in comparison with what I do not know

God's Generals II (The Roaring Performers)
JOHN HUS
IN ROBERTS LIARDON

Humility is truly one mark of a great man. As they say, "No man is an island of knowledge." Humility helps you keep an open mind. However, this openness doesn't mean gullibility.

Truth conquers all

God's Generals II (The Roaring Performers)
JOHN HUS
IN ROBERTS LIARDON

We have learned people who claim that absolute truth doesn't exist. I'm not here to have a philosophical argument with anyone. All I want to say is that absolute truth has proven stronger than any other thing throughout the history of mankind. Go figure that one out. Ravi Zacharias often quotes Andrei Sakharov's conclusion, "I've always thought that the most powerful weapon in the world was the bomb and that's why I gave it to my people, but I've come to the conclusion that the most powerful weapon in the world is not the bomb but it's the truth."

Of this Church if you will be, I cannot hinder you
but as for me, I will be of no other Church
but that which has Jesus Christ for Pastor
hears His voice and will not hear the voice of a stranger

God's Generals II (The Roaring Performers)
JOHN KNOX
IN ROBERTS LIARDON

Christians need to be very careful who they listen to. There are many pastors and preachers in the pulpits today who serve themselves and are answerable to none. Be wise!

Pray. Let God worry

God's Generals II (The Roaring Performers)
MARTIN LUTHER
IN ROBERTS LIARDON

What a simple truth that's so easy to forget. Although it appears easier said than done, it isn't impossible. What's the point of praying when you refuse to release the burden you claim to have dropped with God?

...don't ever underestimate the role you might have
in sowing a seed, or a good deed, into the lives of others
Your action today, when done by the faith and inspiration of God
can powerfully affect the future

God's Generals II (The Roaring Performers)
ROBERTS LIARDON

Don't stop doing good. Keep sowing those precious seeds, even when results aren't immediate. Today's seed might be the saving grace of unborn generations.

In the midst of a disillusioned generation
that has erased the line between right and wrong
In the midst of a world that is dying from its bondage
while thinking it is free
will you stand for the truth (that God is love and still a consuming fire?)

God's Generals II (The Roaring Performers)
ROBERTS LIARDON

When you believe that God is all Love and no Consuming fire, you slide into heresy. The reverse is also true. God is Love to the undeserving sinner in the period of His Grace, and a Consuming fire to the unrepentant sinner in the period of His Just Judgement.

Truth is not relative. Truth is absolute

God's Generals II (The Roaring Performers)
ROBERTS LIARDON

If truth isn't a fixed point, what reference do you use to discern your position in life? No wonder our world is speedily and smilingly drifting into an abyss.

Religion works in the realm of ignorance. . .
It bases its facts on thoughts, legends and what denominations dream up. . .

God's Generals II (The Roaring Performers)
ROBERTS LIARDON

Christianity isn't a religion in the literal sense. It is more of a relationship with Christ; a continuous transformation into His likeness. As such, a Church is the congregation of Christians with Christ as their head.

Apostolic people aren't "peacekeepers"
like those who forsake principles and truth in order to keep everyone happy
Instead, they are "peacemakers"
ready and willing to take the necessary action for truth to prevail

God's Generals II (The Roaring Performers)
ROBERTS LIARDON

It is possible to have both truth and happiness. However, they must be arranged in the right order. Truth ought to take precedence over happiness. Are you more interested in making people happy than telling them the truth? Think that one over.

Man can encourage, but God gives the Strength

God's Generals II (The Roaring Performers)
ROBERTS LIARDON

No matter how men encourage, you can still fail if God doesn't supply the needed Strength. Don't forget that God has the final say.

Reformers understand that
men can't remedy the evils of society, but changed hearts can and will

---

God's Generals II (The Roaring Performers)
ROBERTS LIARDON

This is the truth which many governments have proved right but are still unwilling to admit or accept. Legislation and policies might create an environment of sanity, but will never disturb the evil lurking within the hearts of citizens. Eventually, this evil finds ways to manifest itself.

Ronald Coase

RONALD COASE

Be wary when someone pulls statistics on you. Vance Havner once said that, "there are three kinds of lies: white lie, black lie and statistics." Data is dumb. However, any puppeteer can make it speak their language of choice.

Russell Conwell

If you are not great before you get the office
You won't be great when you secure it

RUSSELL CONWELL

Success is never an overnight achievement. It is a cumulative progression towards an end goal.

If you wish to be great at all
You must begin where you are and [with] what you are

RUSSELL CONWELL

At times, the weakness and poverty of your present situation can be very demoralizing. However, take those broken pieces as your starting point. After all, there is only one of you. There isn't a double elsewhere to substitute in your place.

S

Sam Walton
Samuel Lee
Stephen Covey
Stephen Covey & David Hatch

Sam Walton

All of us profit from being corrected — if we're corrected in a positive way

Sam Walton: Made in America, p. 180
SAM WALTON WITH JOHN HUEY

The quality of the means must match that of the end. A bad means often ruins a good end.

Some people have crowed a great deal
about all their philanthropy over the years
but too many of these foundations, I suspect
were only begun as tax shelters without much real sense of purpose
Many of them seem to have become very nice places to work
for a small group of folks
who have built up pretty thick crusts of administration and bureaucracy

Sam Walton: Made in America, p. 302-303
SAM WALTON WITH JOHN HUEY

What mortal can truly understand the depths of darkness in a person's mind? 1 Samuel 2:3 tells us that it is only God who can truly weigh our actions.

Samuel Lee

If thou suffer a child to go on in sin unregarded, untaught, unrebuked
and think it is too little to give attention to at first
that sinful folly will be thy scourge in the end
God many times whips an aged parent
by that child that was unwhipped at first

The Conversion of Family Members
SAMUEL LEE

Child training is a divine assignment. Some say that corporal punishment is child abuse. Well, that is true if and when done harshly and with wicked motives. However, I don't think that disciplining a child in wisdom and love is evil. How come the armed forces, in few weeks, beat children into shape who have been wayward for many years under their parents? There is one simple answer: structured discipline. Any discipline without pain and discomfort isn't worth its salt. Many baulk at the word pain, and rightly so. C. S. Lewis said that, "...pain...is [God's] megaphone to rouse a deaf world." This is apt and can be applied to child training. Pain and discomfort are part of living, learning and growing.

Stephen Covey

...utilizing our human capacity
to build on the foundation of generations before us
we have inadvertently become so focused on our building
that we have forgotten the foundation that holds it up
in reaping for so long where we have not sown
perhaps we have forgotten the need to sow

The 7 Habits of Highly Effective People
STEPHEN COVEY

Maintenance is good in its place. However, don't live all your life maintaining the heritage of forbears. What heritage will you leave for future generations?

Proactive people carry their own weather with them
Whether it rains or shines makes no difference to them

The 7 Habits of Highly Effective People
STEPHEN COVEY

You won't accomplish much if your productivity constantly depends on environment. Condition your mind to be stronger than your situations.

In the great literature of all progressive societies, love is a verb
Reactive people make it a feeling

The 7 Habits of Highly Effective People
STEPHEN COVEY

Love which doesn't act is simply a fantasy. You love by doing, not just feeling. The feeling might be a by-product but not the main thing.

The process is as important as the product

The 7 Habits of Highly Effective People
Stephen Covey

This is another way of saying that, "The end does not always justify the means." In another sense, what you learn from the process is as important as the product. This is because these lessons could be use to improve subsequent processes and products.

The enemy of the "best" is often the "good"

The 7 Habits of Highly Effective People
Stephen Covey

We have a natural tendency to resist change in general and improvement in particular; especially when things are already working well. However, stagnation doesn't necessarily show up as negative results immediately. Its manifestation can take years.

You can't change the fruit without changing the root

The 7 Habits of Highly Effective People
Stephen Covey

Superficial solutions only address symptoms leaving the disease revving to manifest once again; possibly in worse forms.

The first thing many people think about when they get into trouble
is suing someone...
but defensive minds are neither creative nor cooperative

The 7 Habits of Highly Effective People
Stephen Covey

Our society frolics in litigation; and many lawyers are tools in the hands of the well-to-do. This has made us a very combative set of people who rarely follow peace with our fellow men.

Unexpressed feelings never die
they're buried alive and come forth later in uglier ways

The 7 Habits of Highly Effective People
STEPHEN COVEY

Make sure you're always true to yourself. Hypocrisy doesn't only affect the other. You might be its worst victim.

An agreement means very little in letter
without the character and relationship base to sustain it in spirit

The 7 Habits of Highly Effective People
STEPHEN COVEY

Few today use their word as their bond. People still can't get along despite the volumes of legal fine-prints available. We really need to shift emphasis from a personality-base to a character-base in our interactions.

The whole is greater than the sum of its parts

The 7 Habits of Highly Effective People
STEPHEN COVEY

This is another way of saying that, "There is power in unity." United effort has a multiplier effect on individual efforts. It goes beyond a simple addition.

The person who is truly effective has the humility and reverence to recognize his own perceptual limitation and to appreciate the rich resources available through interaction with the hearts and minds of other human beings

The 7 Habits of Highly Effective People
STEPHEN COVEY

Greatness without humility is disastrous. It can quickly morph into tyranny.

A person who doesn't read
is no better off than the person who can't read

The 7 Habits of Highly Effective People
STEPHEN COVEY

Your skill is useless if you don't or can't exercise it. It quickly depreciates in that dormant condition.

I believe that a life of integrity
is the most fundamental source of personal worth

The 7 Habits of Highly Effective People
Stephen Covey

Integrity doesn't necessarily translate to success in the literal sense. Also, it has little to with talent or skill. However, it is intricately tied to character: that trait of the real man. It is not that façade of personality, that thin veneer which can be learned and often borders on hypocrisy.

... There are parts to human nature
that cannot be reached by either legislation or education
but require the power of God to deal with

The 7 Habits of Highly Effective People
Stephen Covey

Many world governments who went against this fact recorded pitiful failure. In fact, education might end up equipping a man with the skills to invent ways of increasing evil in the world. Man isn't just a physical being; he is a spiritual being as well. In reality, the spiritual determines the physical. Ponder this one carefully.

One hundred years from now
it will not matter what kind of car I drove
what kind of house I lived in
how much money I had in my bank account
nor what my clothes looked like
But the world may be a little better
because I was important in the life of a child

The 8th Habit
Anonymous
in Stephen Covey

Never underestimate the potential of investing into a child's life. You never can tell what gems and pearls lie hidden there. I truly admire those mothers and fathers who take out time to instil virtues in their children.

With proper training and encouragement, no man can tell what that child could accomplish.

We are a product of our decisions not our conditions

The 8th Habit
ARISTOTLE
IN STEPHEN COVEY

Although conditions might determine our starting point(s) in life, it is still our decisions which determine where we end up. These decisions are the sum of our responses to the conditions we meet in life.

All that is necessary for the triumph of evil is that good men do nothing

The 8th Habit
EDMUND BURKE
IN STEPHEN COVEY

Don't keep quiet when you see evil being done. It might not directly affect you now, but what of others? In fact, evil might eventually catch up with you or your progeny after it becomes a norm in the society.

Back of every noble life
there are principles that have fashioned it

The 8th Habit
GEORGE H. LORIMER
IN STEPHEN COVEY

Principles are like anchors which prevent us from drifting into deep waters. Society may change over time but true principles don't. Also, principles aren't relative. If they aren't absolute, why are they principles? Their absoluteness is what makes them cross-cultural.

No horse gets anywhere until he is harnessed
No steam or gas ever drives anything until it is confined
No Niagara is ever turned into light and power until it is tunneled
No life ever grows great until it is focused, dedicated, disciplined

The 8th Habit
Henry Emerson Fosdick
in Stephen Covey

Don't dream of greatness if you are unwilling to befriend focus, dedication and discipline. These will enable you stick it out through frustrations and challenges.

In vain do they talk of happiness
who never subdued an impulse in obedience to a principle
He who never sacrificed a present for future good
or a personal to a general one
can speak of happiness only as the blind speak of colour

The 8th Habit
Horace Mann
in Stephen Covey

Happiness unhinged from principles is simply indulgence. Today, principles look like what old people reminisce on. Many in my generation pay lip service to principles and use them as cloak for their dubiousness. Success gotten through unprincipled means is a mirage. Eventually, it will be seen for its worth by present generations or (and) the ones yet unborn.

The end of education
is to see men made whole both in competence and in conscience
For to create the power of competence
without creating a corresponding direction
to guide the use of that power is bad education
Furthermore, competence will finally disintegrate apart from conscience

The 8th Habit
John Sloan Dickey
in Stephen Covey

Words for the wise! There are many who see morality as repressive, view God as the creation of man's imagination and desire education to be as atheistic as can be. Unfortunately, some of them are unaware that they're passionately preparing citizens who will bring about the eventual collapse of society.

Most powerful is he who has himself in his power

The 8ᵗʰ Habit
LUCIUS AMAEUS SENECA
IN STEPHEN COVEY

Victory over oneself is key. Apostle Paul said in Romans 6:16 and I paraphrase, "a man is a slave to whatsoever he yields his control." If you have little control over your feelings, then they are your masters.

Anger is an acid
that can do more harm to the vessel in which it stands
than to anything on which it is poured

The 8ᵗʰ Habit
MAHATMA GHANDI
IN STEPHEN COVEY

If you're already hurt by someone, staying angry at that person adds more hurt. Please be wise. No one said forgiveness is an easy task.

Whatever weakens your reason
impairs the tenderness of your conscience
obscures your sense of God
takes off your relish for spiritual things
whatever increases authority of the body over the mind
that thing is sin to you
however innocent it may seem in itself

The 8ᵗʰ Habit
SUSANNA WESLEY
IN STEPHEN COVEY

Not everything which has the approval of the majority is virtuous. Also, not everything done by good men is appropriate for you at a particular moment. Live such that you won't be ashamed to account for your life when it ends.

Education is a progressive discovery of our own ignorance

The 8th Habit
Will Durant
in Stephen Covey

Education goes beyond the acquisition of knowledge. One lacks education if he's not constantly weighing his life on the scale of his current knowledge. Education ought to help you sincerely question your assumptions and presuppositions in life. After all, anything which cannot stand genuine scrutiny wasn't true in the first place. However it is not, and I repeat, it is not a cynical tearing down of your untested beliefs in the first round of questioning.

To every man there comes in his lifetime
that special moment when he is figuratively tapped on the shoulder
and offered a chance to do a very special thing
unique to him and fitted to his talents
What a tragedy if that moment finds him
unprepared or unqualified for the work which would be his finest hour

The 8th Habit
Winston Churchill
in Stephen Covey

You never know when or in what form your ultimate opportunity in life will come. Therefore, be prepared at all times.

Never be blinded by the knowledge that you have

The 8th Habit
Stephen Covey

Knowledge without humility is a fast route to narcissism. It prevents someone from growing any further than his current level.

Become an island of excellence in a sea of mediocrity

The 8th Habit
Stephen Covey

There is always a sea of mediocrity floating around as the majority. Don't set your personal standards based on the prevalent norms. Since we're all unique, you might be cheating yourself by comparing yourself to others. Instead, compare yourself to the potential God placed in you.

Setbacks are inevitable; misery is a choice
There are always reasons, never an excuse

The 8th Habit
STEPHEN COVEY

Don't dwell on your challenges. Learn the available lessons, evaluate your options, and forge ahead. Don't play the blame game. Keep trying and never give up.

All things are created twice

The 8th Habit
STEPHEN COVEY

This is another of saying that your mind is the first realm of creation. What you can't visualise within can't be manifested without. Man isn't just a collection of flesh and bones. He is also a spiritual being.

What is common sense is not common practice

The 8th Habit
STEPHEN COVEY

Until we stop acting on mere feelings and guide our feelings with moral reasoning, this kind of hypocrisy will continue.

Mind over mattress

The 8th Habit
STEPHEN COVEY

There are times when you ought to ignore the legitimate call of sleep. Sleep has never brought progress to any person or society. Train your mind till it can resist the temptation of the mattress.

Stephen Covey & David Hatch

If you want a place in the sun
you've got to put up with a few blisters

Everyday Greatness
ABIGAIL VAN BUREN
IN STEPHEN COVEY & DAVID HATCH

As they say, "There is no free lunch." You need to count the cost before embarking on any worthwhile endeavour.

Success isn't a result of spontaneous combustion
You must set yourself on fire

Everyday Greatness
ARNOLD H. GLASOW
IN STEPHEN COVEY & DAVID HATCH

Success is never by accident. It doesn't happen all of a sudden. It typically involves deliberate effort. Others might spur you into action, but it takes personal determination to achieve your goal.

If you want to leave footprints in the sands of time
don't drag your feet

Everyday Greatness
ARNOT L. SHEPPARD
IN STEPHEN COVEY & DAVID HATCH

This is a very interesting way of expressing this truth. Dragging your feet could mean being lazy or lacking focus in life. Also, it could mean doing worthless things. Today is the right time to evaluate your life in light of this statement. What do you want to be remembered for?

Pay attention to your enemies
for they are the first to discover your mistakes

Everyday Greatness
Antisthenes
in Stephen Covey & David Hatch

This is a tough one to practice because we tend to believe (and for good reasons) that our antagonists are out to get us. However, we ought to see them as free sources of critical review. Check if there is an iota of truth in their statements before dismissing them as irrelevant.

None are so empty as those who are full of themselves

Everyday Greatness
Benjamin Whichcote
in Stephen Covey & David Hatch

Anyone who is so full of himself has no space to learn new things or time to be of help to others. He eventually loses touch with reality.

One man cannot hold another down in the ditch
without remaining down in the ditch with him

Everyday Greatness
Booker T. Washington
in Stephen Covey & David Hatch

Oppression has a way of oppressing the oppressor. Quite an important point to note. Unfortunately, it is easy to forget in the heat of the moment. Let us keep a careful watch over our lives.

I will permit no man to narrow and degrade my soul by making me hate him

Everyday Greatness
Booker T. Washington
in Stephen Covey & David Hatch

Hatred has a way of degrading the hater's soul. It doesn't matter what others have done. You have the power to forgive, even the unworthy. Forgiveness has a cleansing and liberating effect on your soul. Although it is easier said than done, we ought to live above hatred.

A problem well stated is a problem half solved

Everyday Greatness
Charles F. Kettering
in Stephen Covey & David Hatch

Clarity is the first step to solving a problem. If you don't understand a problem, then the first problem to solve is your lack of understanding.

A man who trims himself to suit everybody will soon whittle himself away

Everyday Greatness
Charles Schwab
in Stephen Covey & David Hatch

Settle this beforehand. Despite your best intentions, you can't please everyone. One reason being that there are some whose satisfaction is hinged on your violation of principles. On the other hand, you can't do good to everyone who deserves it. You can only effectively do good to those in your circle of influence. Why not start there today?

In the midst of great joy, do not promise anyone anything
In the midst of great anger, do not answer anyone's letter

Everyday Greatness
Chinese Proverb
in Stephen Covey & David Hatch

This helps you avoid making promises you can't fulfil and saying things you can't unsay.

You can't get ahead while you are getting even

Everyday Greatness
Dick Armey
in Stephen Covey & David Hatch

You decide. Do you want to be stuck at your offenders' level or to forgive them and move ahead? Vance Havner, speaking of Moses' initial attempt to deliver the Israelites from Egyptian bondage said and I paraphrase, "You can't do it cross-eyed." No man makes much progress constantly looking over their shoulders or sideways. In a sense, revenge is a distraction.

You don't get harmony when everybody sings the same note

Everyday Greatness
DOUG FLOYD
IN STEPHEN COVEY & DAVID HATCH

Harmony doesn't necessarily equate to uniformity. Rather, it suggests the attainment of resolved tension. It shows how sometime opposing forces can unite to produce something beautiful. Marriage is one good example.

The search for a scapegoat is the easiest of all human expeditions

Everyday Greatness
DWIGHT EISENHOWER
IN STEPHEN COVEY & DAVID HATCH

We're naturally averse to taking responsibility when things go wrong. However, that is not the way to grow in life.

Truly great men and women are never terrifying
Their humility puts you at ease

Everyday Greatness
ELIZABETH GOUDGE
IN STEPHEN COVEY & DAVID HATCH

One key mark of true greatness is humility. It's alarming that humility is becoming a scarce virtue among many of the world's present greats.

Even a small star shines in the darkness

Everyday Greatness
FINNISH PROVERB
IN STEPHEN COVEY & DAVID HATCH

Don't cover your star no matter how little it is. Help others through this blinding darkness around us. Keep it shining while you work on making it bigger and brighter.

Write injuries in the sand, kindnesses in marble

Everyday Greatness
FRENCH PROVERB
IN STEPHEN COVEY & DAVID HATCH

This is a good recipe for a healthy mind. It frees you of resentment and hatred. Also, it keeps you humble and grateful.

Luxury consist in having time to spare

Everyday Greatness
GONTRAN DE PONCIS
IN STEPHEN COVEY & DAVID HATCH

What a fine way to put it! One might have riches and wealth without any time to spare for any other thing. Therefore, that person has little luxury. However, luxury could be a good or bad thing depending on its use.

Swift gratitude is the sweetest

Everyday Greatness
GREEK PROVERB
IN STEPHEN COVEY & DAVID HATCH

In other words, it is a dish best served hot. Although cooled gratitude is better than nothing, it doesn't warm the heart as much.

Well begun is half-done

Everyday Greatness
GREEK PROVERB
IN STEPHEN COVEY & DAVID HATCH

A well laid foundation will need little or no repairs in future. However, a well finished edifice is the ultimate. A man might begin well but end poorly, or not finish at all. Also, a man might begin poorly but finish well. However, the best is to begin well, stay strong on the course and finish well.

The most important work you and I will ever do
will be within the walls of our own homes

Everyday Greatness
Harold B. Lee
in Stephen Covey & David Hatch

Quite a statement! We have so enlarged our rights as a society to the point that irresponsibility has become a virtue. How many spouses today are willing to settle their difference in the comfort of their homes rather than in divorce courts? How many parents are willing to spend time imparting solid virtues and principles to their children? Unfortunately, we have become am entertainment-obsessed, money-possessed and self-infatuated society. I'm not exempted from this verdict at all. We need to fortify our dilapidated homes into castles that will endure for generations to come.

I say beware of all enterprises that require new clothes
and not rather a new wearer of clothes

Everyday Greatness
Henry David Thoreau
in Stephen Covey & David Hatch

It is the man and not his appearance that makes a difference in society. External and superficial improvements in society will eventually wear off to expose the deficient core of its citizens.

A man without mirth is like a wagon without springs
He is jolted disagreeably by every pebble in the road

Everyday Greatness
Henry Ward Beecher
in Stephen Covey & David Hatch

Laughter is a shock absorber on the rocky road of life. You might make it to your destination without it; but with excruciating pain and avoidable discomfort. It isn't wise to take yourself too seriously all the time. When last did you laugh at yourself?

He who cannot dance puts the blame on the floor

Everyday Greatness
Hindi Proverb
in Stephen Covey & David Hatch

Consider this properly before playing the blame game. We are often to blame and not any external entity.

Success without honour is an unseasoned dish
It will satisfy your hunger but it won't taste good

Everyday Greatness
Joe Paterno
in Stephen Covey & David Hatch

Honour differentiates "good" from "bad" success. Not everything people call success is actually good. What good is a success achieved through immoral means? How can a dishonourable fellow claim to have succeeded in life while leaving a trail of tears and pain behind?

When love and skill work together; expect a masterpiece

Everyday Greatness
John Ruskin
in Stephen Covey & David Hatch

Love as used here encompasses passion, discipline, determination and diligence. Skill as used here means talent, gift and the like. Skill isn't enough. It must be combined with other key ingredients to achieve greatness. As John Maxwell will say, "Talent is never enough."

Values have been carved on monuments
and spelled out in illuminated manuscripts
We do not need more of that
They must be made to live in the acts of men

Everyday Greatness
John W. Gardner
in Stephen Covey & David Hatch

As they say, "Talk is cheap". Saying something is one thing. Practising it is another thing. Does your profession match your practice? This is the right time to confirm.

The glory of great men should always be measured
by the means they have used to acquire it

Everyday Greatness
Le Rouchefoucauld
in Stephen Covey & David Hatch

As they say, "The end does not always justify the means" and "The means determines the end." In light of this, how many of the so-called greats of yesterday and today were great in the real sense? This is worthy of sober reflection.

He who truly knows has no occasion to shout

Everyday Greatness
Leonardo Da Vinci
in Stephen Covey & David Hatch

True knowledge needs no publicity stunt to be heard. If it does, it ceases to be true. Truth is usually the target of the masses' hatred. However, it is found and appreciated by sincere seekers.

Never seem more learned than the people you are with
Wear your learning like a pocket-watch and keep it hidden
Do not pull it out to count the hours, but give the time when you are asked

---

Everyday Greatness
Lord Chesterfield
in Stephen Covey & David Hatch

Any education that doesn't teach a man humility is deformation. The natural pride which comes with much learning ought to be counterbalanced by a greater dose of humility.

Chance favours the prepared mind

Everyday Greatness
Louis Pasteur
in Stephen Covey & David Hatch

If you think people achieve greatness by mere chance, think again. Although some inherit the dividends of their forbears' greatness, that greatness isn't still theirs. None achieves greatness without preparing for that unknown time when opportunity or chance will knock.

Resentment is like taking poison and waiting for the other person to die

---

Everyday Greatness
Malachy McCourt
in Stephen Covey & David Hatch

There are certain things that aren't worth it. Unforgiveness is one of them. It adds more pain to the wrong others have done to you.

We are not held back by the love we didn't receive in the past
but by the love we're not extending in the present

Everyday Greatness
Marianne Williamson
in Stephen Covey & David Hatch

Let's learn to forgive. Forgiveness empowers the forgiver. It emancipates him to be a blessing to others. Although it's easier said than done, it's worth the price.

Intelligence is like a river
the deeper it is, the less noise it makes

Everyday Greatness
Milwaukee Journal Sentinel
in Stephen Covey & David Hatch

Don't get carried away with all the promotional hype in the media about how intelligent this person is and the other person is. If the virtues of modesty and humility aren't bodyguards to intelligence, you'll end up with narcissism.

There is more to life than increasing its speed

Everyday Greatness
MOHANDAS K. GHANDI
IN STEPHEN COVEY & DAVID HATCH

Life can be lived at so fast a pace to leave no print on the sands of time. Do you at least take time to observe or appreciate the scenes you're zooming past in life?

If you're not learning while you're earning
you're cheating yourself out of the better portion of your compensation

---

Everyday Greatness
NAPOLEON HILL
IN STEPHEN COVEY & DAVID HATCH

Once you stop learning, you start stunting. It doesn't matter how much money is coming into your account; because, others who keep learning won't wait for you. You begin retrogressing relative to these learners, and that flow of money will eventually divert to the learners.

Listen or thy tongue will keep thee deaf

Everyday Greatness
NATIVE AMERICAN PROVERB
IN STEPHEN COVEY & DAVID HATCH

As they say, "God gave man two ears and one tongue for a reason." Talkativeness has a way of deafening a man. It's a slippery slope towards narcissism since that man would rather hear himself than listen to others.

Wherever we look upon this earth
the opportunities take shape within the problems

Everyday Greatness
NELSON A. ROCKEFELLER
IN STEPHEN COVEY & DAVID HATCH

Be a solution provider: that go-to person people consult when problems arise.

Most of us would rather be ruined by praise than saved by criticism

Everyday Greatness
Norman Vincent Peale
in Stephen Covey & David Hatch

We need to be deliberate in accepting criticism. Weigh your life against constructive ones and adjust accordingly. Weigh your life against destructive ones and forgive accordingly.

The mass of men worry themselves into nameless graves
while here and there
a great unselfish soul forgets himself into immortality

Everyday Greatness
Ralph Waldo Emerson
in Stephen Covey & David Hatch

What are you doing that is greater than yourself? Are you living in light of eternity? Selfishness has never taken anyone beyond himself.

Bad times have a scientific value
These are occasions a good learner would not miss

Everyday Greatness
Ralph Waldo Emerson
in Stephen Covey & David Hatch

Make every situation in life a learning experience. You learn how to avoid repeating the same mistakes. You learn more about yourself. You learn how to encourage and comfort those will later pass through similar experiences.

Hot heads and cold hearts never solved anything

Everyday Greatness
Rev. Billy Graham
in Stephen Covey & David Hatch

Stubbornness and apathy will most likely worsen a situation. So pause a while and evaluate your motives before acting. Are you passionate about any cause? This might be the time to get some.

Most people are willing to pay more to be amused than to be educated

Everyday Greatness
ROBERT C. SAVAGE
IN STEPHEN COVEY & DAVID HATCH

Isn't this an interesting observation? Our obsession with social media and entertainment today is almost out of hand. When was the last time you forwent amusement to learn something new and productive?

When a man does not know what harbor he is making for
no wind is the right wind

Everyday Greatness
SENECA
IN STEPHEN COVEY & DAVID HATCH

Why bother with the journey if you have no destination; since every step leads nowhere? With no vision, there is no mission.

In matters of principle, stand like a rock
In matters of taste, swim with the current

Everyday Greatness
THOMAS JEFFERSON
IN STEPHEN COVEY & DAVID HATCH

Worthwhile living requires a resistance to spirit of the times and a rooting in timeless principles. Although a man ought to be flexible while interacting with others, this flexibility shouldn't exceed the bounds of principles. It is easy to buy into the lie that truth is non-existent or relative. This is because it frees us to conscienceless selfishness.

Nothing gives one person so much advantage over another
as to remain always cool and unruffled under all circumstances

Everyday Greatness
THOMAS JEFFERSON
IN STEPHEN COVEY & DAVID HATCH

This coolness isn't apathy. Quietness in turbulence is a precious trait. As they say, "Silence is golden." It minimizes your predictability; and keeps agitators guessing and second-guessing your next move.

Even if you're on the right track
you'll get run over if you just sit there

Everyday Greatness
WILL ROGERS
IN STEPHEN COVEY & DAVID HATCH

Keep moving forward. A little step in the path of greatness is better than none. Remember, others won't pause their march to greatness just because you're sitting by the road.

Adversity causes some men to break, others to break records

Everyday Greatness
WILLIAM ARTHUR WARD
IN STEPHEN COVEY & DAVID HATCH

The second part complements the quote which says that "Necessity is the mother of invention." How do you respond to adversity?

Act upon life
Attach yourself to meaningful, uplifting purposes
Live in accordance with timeless, universal principles

Everyday Greatness
STEPHEN COVEY & DAVID HATCH

Don't be a bystander or onlooker in life. You're meant to be a participant. Do something meaningful with your life. However, ensure that your deeds are guided by right principles such as truth, justice and love.

Cliché or not
we just don't know how blessed we are until misfortune strikes

Everyday Greatness
STEPHEN COVEY & DAVID HATCH

Learn to appreciate those around you. Be grateful for the much you have. You never can tell what tomorrow may bring.

Part of achieving happiness is learning to enjoy
even the less invigorating parts of the journey

Everyday Greatness
STEPHEN COVEY & DAVID HATCH

Happiness isn't necessarily a destination. Often, it is more of our attitude towards life's circumstances.

A complementary team is one
where strengths are made productive and weaknesses are made irrelevant

---

Everyday Greatness
STEPHEN COVEY & DAVID HATCH

Although this has broad applications, it poignantly reminds me of marriage. Marriage is meant for a man and woman, who despite their often opposing biological proclivities, can form a united force. This doesn't mean that their individual weaknesses cease to exist. Rather, they are humble and diligent enough to function in a way that maximizes the impacts of each person's strengths and minimizes the consequences of each person's weaknesses.

Charity is love in work clothes

Everyday Greatness
STEPHEN COVEY & DAVID HATCH

Charity that costs you nothing is fake. Most of this noise about charity today are simply public relations stunts. Often, true charity isn't glamorous and attention seeking.

T

Thomas Brooks
Thomas Friedman
Thomas Manton
Thomas Paine
Tim Lahaye
Timothy Keller

Thomas Brooks

Charitable Christians are as wise merchants, happy usurers
parting with that which they cannot keep
that they may gain that which they cannot lose

The Complete Works of Thomas Brooks, Vol. 3
Epistle Dedicatory, A Cabinet of Jewels, p. 245
THOMAS BROOKS

Do you give to others and good causes even when it is inconvenient? Make this part of your eternal, investment strategy.

We must live soberly in respect of ourselves
righteously in respect of our neighbours
and godly in respect of God
And this is the sum of a Christian's whole duty

The Complete Works of Thomas Brooks, Vol. 3
A Cabinet of Jewels, p. 313
THOMAS BROOKS

We have three key words: soberness, righteousness and godliness. Soberness is much needed today, when it's very hard to differentiate Christians from non-Christians on the basis of appearance and comportment.

Walking in the power of holiness
lies much in shunning the very appearance of sin

The Complete Works of Thomas Brooks, Vol. 3
A Cabinet of Jewels, p. 324
THOMAS BROOKS

The more grace any man hath in his own heart
the more fearful he will be of stumbling or offending those that have less

The Complete Works of Thomas Brooks, Vol. 3
A Cabinet of Jewels, p. 324
THOMAS BROOKS

Holiness produces a deep spiritual sensitivity in man, which helps him err on the side of caution in his daily living.

Such as have most pampered their bodies
have been the greatest enemies to their own souls...
he is certainly an unhappy man whose outside is his best side

The Complete Works of Thomas Brooks, Vol. 3
A Cabinet of Jewels, p. 351-352
THOMAS BROOKS

How is your heart? Is it as pure and holy as your physical appearance? Do you even take time to feed your soul through spiritual exercises like personal Bible study, spiritual songs and prayers?

Grace will make your names immortal...
Wicked men many times outlive their names
but the names of just men outlive them

The Complete Works of Thomas Brooks, Vol. 3
A Cabinet of Jewels, p. 366-367
THOMAS BROOKS

Don't be among that crowd with messy lives whose names have or will become epitomes of evil. Live such that friends and foes will feel an emptiness when you're gone. Let your life count both for now and in eternity.

Holy zeal is a fire that will make its way through all things
that stands between God and the soul...
Only remember this, though zeal should eat up our sins
yet it must not eat up our wisdom
no more than policy should eat up our zeal

The Complete Works of Thomas Brooks, Vol. 3
A Cabinet of Jewels, p. 400
THOMAS BROOKS

Zeal must be circumscribed by wisdom. Similarly, we shouldn't quench our zeal in the name of policy and diplomacy; a diplomacy which is the younger sibling to hypocrisy.

Man by nature is a vain-glorious creature
apt to boast and brag of the sins that he is free of
but unwilling to confess the sins that he is guilty of

The Complete Works of Thomas Brooks, Vol. 3
A Cabinet of Jewels, p. 404
THOMAS BROOKS

What an insight! Christian, humility is indispensable every time you come before the Word of God: in private devotion or public worship. Else, you will be caught in this fine web of self-delusion.

… dissembled sanctity is double iniquity

The Complete Works of Thomas Brooks, Vol. 3
A Cabinet of Jewels, p. 437
THOMAS BROOKS

It is one thing to commit iniquity. It is quite another thing to cover your iniquity with a façade of sanctity. This way, you can even deceive the righteous and cause much havoc in the Church.

The emptiest barrels make the loudest sound
the worst metal the greatest noise
and the lightest ears of corn hold their heads highest

The Complete Works of Thomas Brooks, Vol. 3
A Cabinet of Jewels, p. 451
THOMAS BROOKS

Notice several key concepts here: emptiness, lightness and loudness. Someone might not be empty and yet full of chaff, making great noise all the way. How can a Christian purge these from his life without daily examination before God's Word?

Faith makes the soul fruitful
Faith hath Rachel's eye and Leah's womb

The Complete Works of Thomas Brooks, Vol. 1
Appendix to Memoir, p. xlii-xliii
Thomas Brooks

Faith produces radiant beauty and abundant fruitfulness.

Where faith is wanting, men's souls will be like the cypress
the more it is watered, the more it is withered

The Complete Works of Thomas Brooks, Vol. 1
Appendix to Memoir, p. xliii
Thomas Brooks

One of Vance Havner's quotes is apt here and I paraphrase: "...light is useless where there is no sight ... people can be blinded by lack of sight or too much light..." Faith is the catalyst which activates the Word of God that a man hears. Continual hearing without faith hardens the hearer and desensitize his conscience till it eventually works death in him.

Though true repentance be never too late, yet late repentance is seldom true

---

The Complete Works of Thomas Brooks, Vol. 1
Apples of Gold, p. 190
Thomas Brooks

Postponing the day of repentance is dangerous since death doesn't often knock before entering the house.

Well! young men, remember this
clothes and company do often times tell tales
in a mute but significant language

The Complete Works of Thomas Brooks, Vol. 1
Apples of Gold, p. 247
Thomas Brooks

This message is for everyone, not just young men. We need to watch our appearance and acquaintances. A Christianity which can't influence our appearance and choice of close associates ought to questioned. There

is a big problem if others can't sense something of Christ in you without
your declaration.

...precepts may instruct, but examples do persuade

The Complete Works of Thomas Brooks, Vol. 2
Epistle Dedicatory to Heaven on Earth, p. 308
THOMAS BROOKS

One hymn writer put it this way, "...prove it by the life you live."
Another says, "...your life's a book before their eyes, they're reading it
through and through ...do others see Jesus in you?" Ensure your profession and practice are consistent.

Prosperity makes friends, and adversity will try friends

The Complete Works of Thomas Brooks, Vol. 2
Heaven on Earth, p. 486
THOMAS BROOKS

It is very easy to make friends when you have material wealth. You
only know the true ones in turbulent times.

Extremes in government are the ready way to ruin all...
Extreme right often proves extreme wrong
He that will always go to the utmost of what the law allows
will too too often do more than the law requires
A rigid severity often mars all
Equity is still to be preferred before extremity

The Complete Works of Thomas Brooks, Vol. 6
The Epistle Dedicatory, London's Lamentations, p. 5
THOMAS BROOKS

A timely warning for all in positions of authority and power: parents,
pastors, politicians and the rest.

Stars shine brightest in the darkest night
Torches are the better for beating
Grapes come not to the proof till they come to the press
Spices smell sweetest when pounded
Young trees root the faster for shaking
Vines are the better for bleeding
Gold looks the brighter for scouring
and juniper smells sweetest in the fire

The Complete Works of Thomas Brooks, Vol. 6
London's Lamentations, p. 19
Thomas Brooks

If properly handled, adversity could be a chance for productivity and progress.

The explication of a doctrine is but the drawing of the bow
the application is the hitting of the mark, the white...

The Complete Works of Thomas Brooks, Vol. 6
London's Lamentations, p. 128
Thomas Brooks

What good is a well-explained doctrine to people who aren't told how it applies to them? What good is a well-prepared sermon to a man who refuses to apply it in practice?

Many eat that on earth that they digest in hell

The Complete Works of Thomas Brooks, Vol. 1
Precious Remedies Against Satan's Devices, p. 14
Thomas Brooks

Don't envy the robust cheeks and full stomachs of wicked men whose indigestion will soon start. This will keep them belching and farting rottenness till they reach that eternal abode of anguish and no return.

The eye is the window of the soul
and if that should be always open
the soul might smart for it

The Complete Works of Thomas Brooks, Vol. 1
Precious Remedies Against Satan's Devices, p. 40
Thomas Brooks

You might not be in control of what you see, but you can control what you watch. What you watch has a way of moulding your thoughts, behaviour and habit.

He that shooteth at the sun, though he be far short
will shoot higher than he that aimeth at a shrub

The Complete Works of Thomas Brooks, Vol. 1
Precious Remedies Against Satan's Devices, p. 41
THOMAS BROOKS

Don't set goals that won't task you. Set some goals you've not achieved before; then get to work. Stop selling yourself short of your potentials.

It is a sad and dangerous thing
to have two eyes to behold our dignity and privileges
and not one to see our duties and service

The Complete Works of Thomas Brooks, Vol. 1
Precious Remedies Against Satan's Devices, p. 77
THOMAS BROOKS

Rights and responsibilities are usually two sides of a coin. Ignoring the former might degenerate to slavery. Ignoring the latter will result in anarchy.

Thy soul is a jewel more worth than heaven and earth

The Complete Works of Thomas Brooks, Vol. 1
Precious Remedies Against Satan's Devices, p. 85
THOMAS BROOKS

Take time to ponder over this one. A man never really dies in terms of cessation of consciousness. Your soul will be alive after heaven and earth have passed away. Jesus Christ made this point in Matthew 16:26, Mark 8:36 and Luke 9:25 respectively.

The fuller the vessel is of wine, the less room there is for water

The Complete Works of Thomas Brooks, Vol. 1
Precious Remedies Against Satan's Devices, p. 89
THOMAS BROOKS

How much wine of truth and grace are you filled with? Has the water of frivolities began to nudge some of these out of your life?

The world was once destroyed with water for the heat of lusts
it is thought it will be again destroyed with fire for the coldness of love

The Complete Works of Thomas Brooks, Vol. 1
Precious Remedies Against Satan's Devices, p. 130
Thomas Brooks

Has your love as a Christian grown cold? Do you still relish reading and meditating on the Scriptures? Do you still love the fellowship of true brethren? Do you still love your fellow men, even the problem makers?

...though faith be the champion of grace, and love the nurse of grace
yet humility is the beautifier of grace
it casts a general glory upon all the graces in the soul

The Complete Works of Thomas Brooks, Vol. 1
Precious Remedies Against Satan's Devices, p. 136
Thomas Brooks

Faith gives grace a militant edge and love nurtures it. However, humility is what beautifies this militancy and love, even in the eyes of unbelievers.

He that will play with Satan's bait
will quickly be taken with Satan's hook

The Complete Works of Thomas Brooks, Vol. 1
Precious Remedies Against Satan's Devices, p. 159
Thomas Brooks

This is one way to consider 1 Thessalonians 5:22. No sin or temptation should be underestimated. You never can tell what dark hole it leads to.

...justice is the pulse of a kingdom

The Complete Works of Thomas Brooks, Vol. 4
Epistle Dedicatory to The Crown and Glory of Christianity, p. 8
Thomas Brooks

This is how it ought to be. However, there are many kingdoms which call good evil and evil good; that deny justice to the innocent or delay it till he gives up.

And the Scythian philosopher hath long since complained
that laws were like spiders' webs
that would take flies but not wasps or hornets

The Complete Works of Thomas Brooks, Vol. 4
Epistle Dedicatory to The Crown and Glory of Christianity, p. 9
THOMAS BROOKS

This is what happens where you have unjust lawmakers, deceptive laws and evil judges. Those of low status are closely checked while those of means often find "loopholes." One prime example is most tax laws today.

...many preachers in these days...
have good lungs, but bad brains and worse hearts and lives...

The Complete Works of Thomas Brooks, Vol. 4
Epistle Dedicatory to The Crown and Glory of Christianity, p. 24
THOMAS BROOKS

Unfortunately, this is still the case today. Shouting the message of Salvation from the pulpit or street corner wouldn't cut it. A preacher, or even a Christian should ensure his practice doesn't negate his preaching. He must daily examine himself under the Light of Scriptures, irrespective of commendations from friends and foes.

The sword of the Spirit never wounds deep
till it be plucked out of the gaudy scabbards of human eloquence

The Complete Works of Thomas Brooks, Vol. 4
Epistle Dedicatory to The Crown and Glory of Christianity, p. 24
THOMAS BROOKS

Don't blunt God's Grace with your God-given gifts. Gifts are good but should be tools and servants not exhibits and masters.

A preacher's life should be a commentary upon his doctrine
his practice should be the counterpane of his sermons

The Complete Works of Thomas Brooks, Vol. 4
Epistle Dedicatory to The Crown and Glory of Christianity, p. 24
Thomas Brooks

This is another way of saying, "Practice what you preach." It is very easy to teach what we don't practice or are unwilling to obey. Hypocrisy comes in different shades.

Better is holiness without peace, than peace without holiness

The Complete Works of Thomas Brooks, Vol. 4
Epistle Dedicatory to The Crown and Glory of Christianity, p. 37
Thomas Brooks

Holiness and peace aren't necessarily mutually exclusive. However, are you willing to suffer for holiness' sake than to give up holiness for peace's sake? Are you ready to be hated, abused and scorned by family, friends and foes for holiness' sake? Don't sell holiness at the price of pleasing anyone or anything.

Men of greatest gifts are not always men of greatest holiness. . .
Gifts without holiness will but make a man twice [f]old the child of hell

The Complete Works of Thomas Brooks, Vol. 4
The Crown and Glory of Christianity, p. 92
Thomas Brooks

Gifts are good in their proper place. However, excessive focus on gifts will make a man disdain and neglect growing in grace. This will create rottenness from within, which might not be perceived by others until hope is almost lost.

The greatest scholars have often proved the greatest sinners
the stoutest opposers, and the worst of persecutors

The Complete Works of Thomas Brooks, Vol. 4
The Crown and Glory of Christianity, p. 92-93
Thomas Brooks

A pure heart is better than a golden head

The Complete Works of Thomas Brooks, Vol. 4
The Crown and Glory of Christianity, p. 94
THOMAS BROOKS

Purity of heart is the engine of holy living and peacemaking; which are prerequisites for spending eternity with God. A head sparkling with knowledge might make one renowned on earth and to pridefully disdain others of lower mental abilities. As such, it stirs strife on earth and bars entry into heaven.

...a man that is truly holy can never be holy enough

The Complete Works of Thomas Brooks, Vol. 4
The Crown and Glory of Christianity, p. 107
THOMAS BROOKS

True holiness works a fine sensitivity into a man's conscience. This helps him properly perceive his helplessness to maintain holy living without God's Grace; in this world of temptations.

...holiness is a flower that grows not in nature's garden...
holiness is of a divine offspring

The Complete Works of Thomas Brooks, Vol. 4
The Crown and Glory of Christianity, p. 152
THOMAS BROOKS

The natural man can be disciplined enough to achieve morality but never holiness. Holiness is a gift and grace from God.

The actions of rulers are most commonly rules for the people's actions
and their example passeth as current as their coin

The Complete Works of Thomas Brooks, Vol. 4
The Crown and Glory of Christianity, p. 156
THOMAS BROOKS

Rulers at all levels ought to closely watch their lives to ensure they match the laws, rules and guidelines they make or promote. A public life must be a public light; else, most of the land will be dark.

Many a soul hath been won by the dumb oratory of a holy life

The Complete Works of Thomas Brooks, Vol. 4
The Crown and Glory of Christianity, p. 162
THOMAS BROOKS

As the hymn writer says, "if you say you love the Saviour…prove it by the life you live." It isn't enough to proclaim the Gospel with your mouth while it is hardly discerned in your life.

We are to follow the examples of the best men
not an inch further than they were followers of Christ

The Complete Works of Thomas Brooks, Vol. 4
The Crown and Glory of Christianity, p. 190
THOMAS BROOKS

This is a word of caution to all. Never lift a man to the point where he eclipses your view of Christ. Hebrews 12:2 tells us to keep "looking unto Jesus the author and finisher of our faith…" We should to follow a man only as long as he strictly follows Christ. Never get this mixed up.

Sinful omissions prepare the way to sinful commissions
and both prepare the way to a fatal destruction

The Complete Works of Thomas Brooks, Vol. 4
The Crown and Glory of Christianity, p. 233
THOMAS BROOKS

Our spiritual sensitivity begins to die when we start excusing faults in our lives. Before long, our principles become so low that we approve of things that were previously repulsive to us.

Many persons are only constant in inconstancy

The Complete Works of Thomas Brooks, Vol. 4
The Crown and Glory of Christianity, p. 340
THOMAS BROOKS

Are you so slippery that your word can't be taken as your bond? Are you're so carefree that your promises mean nothing?

. . . but the truth is
he is the best grammarian
that hath learned to speak the truth from his heart
and he is the best astronomer that hath his conversation in heaven
and he is the best musician
that hath learnt practically to sing out the praises of God
and he is the best arithmetician that knows how to number his days
and he is the best read in ethics that every day grows holier and holier
and he is the best skilled in economics
that trains up his family in the fear of the Lord
and he is the best politician
that is as good at taking good counsel as he is at giving good counsel
and he is the best linguist that speaks the language of Canaan. . .

The Complete Works of Thomas Brooks, Vol. 4
The Crown and Glory of Christianity, p. 415
THOMAS BROOKS

Friend, is this a fair description of your lifestyle? If not, what are you waiting for? Today is the best and right day to start working at it.

If Christians are not very much upon their watch
their very callings and offices may prove a very great snare to their souls

---

The Complete Works of Thomas Brooks, Vol. 5
The Golden Key To Open Hidden Treasures, p. 32
THOMAS BROOKS

A Christian's life ought to be one of militant carefulness. Else, his very gift from God can quickly turn into his undoing.

Theory is the guide of practice, and practice is the life of theory

---

The Complete Works of Thomas Brooks, Vol. 1
Epistle Dedicatory to The Mute Christian Under The Smarting Rod, p. 292
THOMAS BROOKS

The Scriptures ought to guide your lifestyle. Your lifestyle ought to be a picture and reflection of the Scriptures. As Marilyn Baker sang, ". . . I love you my children, and I want you to be; a radiant reflection, a living image of me. . ."

Many would wear the crown with Christ
that do not care for bearing the cross with Christ

The Complete Works of Thomas Brooks, Vol. 1
The Mute Christian Under The Smarting Rod, p. 358
Thomas Brooks

There is usually no victory without a battle. As the popular saying goes, and I paraphrase, "...many would love to take Christ as their Saviour but not their Lord."

Temptations may be troubles to my mind
but they are not sins upon my soul whilst I am in arms against them

---

The Complete Works of Thomas Brooks, Vol. 1
The Mute Christian Under The Smarting Rod, p. 366
Thomas Brooks

Temptations might be many things but not sins; so far as they're not yielded to.

As the furnace tries gold
so delays will try what metal a Christian is made of

The Complete Works of Thomas Brooks, Vol. 1
The Mute Christian Under The Smarting Rod, p. 387
Thomas Brooks

This is a truth which may not be truly understood until experienced. Remember that the length of this delay is unknown beforehand.

Godliness never rises to a higher pitch
than when men keep closest to their closets

The Complete Works of Thomas Brooks, Vol. 2
To The Reader, The Privy Key of Heaven, p. 162
Thomas Brooks

Some level of godliness might be attained by attending public worship. However, taking time alone to meditate, pray and read God's Word is one sure way of climbing this "Jacob's ladder."

. . . every man is that really which he is secretly

The Complete Works of Thomas Brooks, Vol. 2
To The Reader, The Privy Key of Heaven, p. 162
THOMAS BROOKS

Hypocrisy can only fool others and even yourself for so long.

Private prayer is a golden key to unlock the mysteries of the Word unto us

The Complete Works of Thomas Brooks, Vol. 2
To The Reader, The Privy Key of Heaven, p. 176
THOMAS BROOKS

Note the word "private." Public worship has in its place but mustn't overshadow your private devotion.

. . . there are two kinds of antidotes against all the troubles of this life
viz. fervent prayers and holy patience
the one hot, the other cold; the one quickening, and the other quenching

The Complete Works of Thomas Brooks, Vol. 2
To The Reader, The Privy Key of Heaven, p. 259
THOMAS BROOKS

Though God seldom comes at our time
yet he never fails to come at his own time

The Complete Works of Thomas Brooks, Vol. 2
To The Reader, The Privy Key of Heaven, p. 277
THOMAS BROOKS

That blessed combination of prayer in all its fervency and patience in all its holiness; with all the tenuous balance between them! Holding the former alone could make a man take offence at God's apparent "delay." Holding the later alone will simply be wishful thinking.

An idle life and an holy heart are far enough asunder
By doing nothing, saith the heathen man, men learn to do evil things

The Complete Works of Thomas Brooks, Vol. 2
To The Reader, The Privy Key of Heaven, p. 278
THOMAS BROOKS

Busyness doesn't equate to productivity. Yet busyness even in a good pastime is better than idleness. Idleness is one sure passport to evil thoughts and unproductive curiosities.

Men rich and strong in grace
look upon this world with a holy scorn and disdain

The Complete Works of Thomas Brooks, Vol. 3
The Unsearchable Riches of Christ, p. 50
THOMAS BROOKS

Souls strong in grace have their feet where carnal men's heads are

The Complete Works of Thomas Brooks, Vol. 3
The Unsearchable Riches of Christ, p. 56
THOMAS BROOKS

Note the words "holy" and "carnal." Although this world offers legitimate comforts and pleasures to a Christian, he mustn't drink them so much as to lose sight of the ultimate.

Zeal without knowledge is a wild-fire in a fool's hand

The Complete Works of Thomas Brooks, Vol. 3
The Unsearchable Riches of Christ, p. 55
THOMAS BROOKS

Zeal is like fire
in the chimney it is one of the best servants
but out of the chimney it is one of the worst masters

The Complete Works of Thomas Brooks, Vol. 3
The Unsearchable Riches of Christ, p. 55
THOMAS BROOKS

Zeal is important in life: spiritually and physically. However, it needs to be guarded. Else, it can perpetrate much evil under the guise of truth.

A man may hear and pray many years
and yet be carnal, base, and worldly as ever

The Complete Works of Thomas Brooks, Vol. 3
The Unsearchable Riches of Christ, p. 129
THOMAS BROOKS

It is not all the talking and profession in the world
that can stop the mouths of foolish men
it must be well-doings
grace improved, grace exercised and manifested in ways of holiness
that must work so great a wonder as to stop the mouths of wicked men

The Complete Works of Thomas Brooks, Vol. 3
The Unsearchable Riches of Christ, p. 144
THOMAS BROOKS

What a timely word of warning to every Christian. Scrutinize your life today. How are you living? Is your practice as beautiful or even more beautiful than your profession?

Frequent acts cause a stronger habit both in graces and in sins

The Complete Works of Thomas Brooks, Vol. 3
The Unsearchable Riches of Christ, p. 180
THOMAS BROOKS

Addiction isn't always a bad thing. Although the picture frequently associated with addiction is negative, it isn't the complete picture. Considering 1 Corinthians 16:15, are you addicted to meditating and studying the Scriptures, loving your fellow men, doing good even to those who hurt you? As they say, "Practice makes perfect."

No one scripture speaks out the whole mind of God; and therefore
you must compare and consult this scripture with the scriptures

The Complete Works of Thomas Brooks, Vol. 3
The Unsearchable Riches of Christ, p. 205
THOMAS BROOKS

Someone said, and I paraphrase, "... taking one part of scripture to an extreme will lead you off a tangent into heresy..." Today is the best day to start your personal Bible study.

Wicked ministers do more hurt by their lives
than they do good by their doctrine

The Complete Works of Thomas Brooks, Vol. 3
The Unsearchable Riches of Christ, p. 217
Thomas Brooks

Every minister's life should be a commentary upon Christ's life

The Complete Works of Thomas Brooks, Vol. 3
The Unsearchable Riches of Christ, p. 217
Thomas Brooks

Ensure that your profession matches your practice. Hypocrisy can be a subtle root of bitterness least perceived by the soil it grows in.

A man high in communion with God
is a man too big for temptations to conquer, or troubles to subdue
Those who have but little communion with God
are usually as soon conquered as tempted, as soon vanquished as assaulted

The Hypocrite Detected, Epistle Dedicatory
Thomas Brooks

A man can ignore God intentionally or unintentionally. The cares of life can so grab his attention that he sets little or no time aside for prayer, praise and prostration before God. A man who ignores God weakens his defences against temptations and troubles.

Thomas Friedman

Out of clutter, find simplicity
From discord, find harmony
In the middle of difficulty, lies opportunity

The World is Flat
ALBERT EINSTEIN
IN THOMAS FRIEDMAN

Often, there are seeds of greatness lying in the midst of all those troubles. Be patient, be observant.

Always tell the truth
that way you won't have to remember what you said

The World is Flat
MARK TWAIN
IN THOMAS FRIEDMAN

Liars need to dedicate a reasonable portion of their memory for storing false data. What a distorted way to live!

To build may have to be the slow and laborious task of years
To destroy can be the thoughtless act of a single day

The World is Flat
SIR WINSTON CHURCHILL
IN THOMAS FRIEDMAN

Treasure every good and worthwhile thing: yours or others. Consider what Apostle Paul said in Philippians 4:8, "Finally, brethren, whatsoever things are true, whatsoever things are honest, whatsoever things are just, whatsoever things are pure, whatsoever things are lovely, whatsoever things are of good report; if there be any virtue, and if there be any praise, think on these things."

Democracy is great
but democracy without responsibility is truly frightening

The World is Flat
THOMAS FRIEDMAN

This speaks to the drive of multiplying rights to the neglect of responsibility in our days. Little wonder we have many respected prodigals in positions of power and authority today.

Thomas Manton

Families are the seminaries of Church and Commonwealth
Religion dwelt first in families
and as they grew into numerous societies
they grew into Churches

Sermon upon Psalm CXXVII.3
THOMAS MANTON

May we never forget this! All this craze of mothers and fathers chasing money and ministry at the expense of their primary God-given assignment is a disgrace to Christianity. Isn't this one of the reasons we're losing the younger generations to atheism, cynicism and all the other "isms"? Mull that one over.

Thomas Paine

A long habit of not thinking a thing wrong
gives it a superficial appearance of being right
and raises at first a formidable outcry in defense of custom
but the tumult soon subsides
Time makes more converts than reason

Common Sense
THOMAS PAINE

This is a warning to those who live according what the majority approves; which isn't always in the right. The majority has often been swindled and brainwashed by sustained propaganda. Consider what Alexander Pope said, "Vice is a monster of so frightful mien; As, to be hated, needs to be seen; Yet seen too oft, familiar with her face; We first endure, then pity, them embrace." Guide and guard your life with time-tested principles; even if you become "part of a lonesome minority" as Vance Havner would say.

Tim Lahaye

You can use your background
as an excuse for present behavior only until you become a Christian
After that it is no longer a valid excuse

I Love You, But Why Are We So Different, Chapter 9, p. 86
DR. HENRY BRANDT
IN TIM LAHAYE

You must take responsibility of unacceptable behaviours. God made provision for you to overcome those weaknesses. This is why I strongly believe that no God-ordained marriage between genuine Christian spouses ought to fail due to incompatibility issues.

The education you receive
whether formal or through voluntary reading and listening
carries a philosophy
and will directly influence your thinking patterns and perspectives

---

I Love You, But Why Are We So Different, Chapter 21, p. 260
TIM LAHAYE

Be deliberate in what you feed your mind. Be very environment conscious since your subconscious doesn't stop absorbing information. These could be background music or discussions in open places like home, mall, airport and office.

Make no mistake about it –
the most important people in the life of any child are his tutor-parents
If they take advantage of their God-given position
in the early years of their children's lives
they can teach the principles...
that no mind-bender can take from them later

Understanding The Male Temperament, Chapter 2, p. 20
TIM LAHAYE

Parents should stop shirking their divine responsibility under any guise. There will always be reasonable excuses to cover up their failings. It could be the desire to leave an inheritance for their children or buy a better house for their upbringing. Nevertheless, there are many pernicious "mind benders" out there. These people could be state-sponsored indoctrinators or even those you pay for daycare.

Timothy Keller

Without the power of grace, truth and love can't be combined

The Meaning of Marriage, Chapter 5, p. 164
TIMOTHY KELLER

We have a natural tendency to veer off into harshness, rashness and pride in the process of upholding truth. On the other hand, we also have a tendency to overlook truth in the name of love.

Marriage has unique power to show us the truth of who we really are

The Meaning of Marriage, Chapter 5, p. 167
TIMOTHY KELLER

At times, people run out of marriage because they can't stand the image in the mirror. This is also a word of caution to the unmarried who desire marriage: start working on your life right away.

V

Vance Havner
Victor Frankl

Vance Havner

Christian = Christ, I am Nothing!

Sermon on 2nd Chronicles 7
VANCE HAVNER

Quite a way to draw our attention to this truth.

Victor Frankl

Everyone has his own specific vocation or mission in life...
Therein he cannot be replaced nor can his life be repeated
Thus, everyone's task is
as unique as is his specific opportunity to implement it

VICTOR FRANKL

Don't unduly compare yourself with others. There's none else like you. As Catherine Marshall put in, "The mold was broken when each of us was born." Therefore, compare yourself to the potential God has placed in you.

W

Walt Whitman
Walter Malone
Warren W. Wiersbe
Watchman Nee
Will Durant
William Booth
William Gairdner
William Gurnall
William James

Walt Whitman

Nothing external to me has any power over me

WALT WHITMAN

External forces can destroy your body but might not be able to touch your soul, i.e. your real self. The mind, which is part of the soul, is a complex fortress given to man by God. It is a defensive and offensive weapon. Never underestimate it.

Walter Malone

Wail not for precious chances passed away
Weep not for golden ages on the wane
Each night I burn the records of the day
At sunrise every soul is born again

WALTER MALONE

You cannot live today by dwelling in yesterday; neither can you march into the future by looking backwards. Do yourself a favour by redeeming today.

Warren W. Wiersbe

Power for holiness and character is first
Power for service is second

50 People Every Christian Should Know, p. 111
ALEXANDER MACLAREN
IN WARREN W. WIERSBE

As someone said, "Power before purity can be disastrous." We really need to get the right order.

When he discovered a truth, he first applied it to himself
and then sought the best way to share it with his people

50 People Every Christian Should Know, p. 111
ALEXANDER MACLAREN
IN WARREN W. WIERSBE

Don't be too eager to teach others what you've not practised or you're not practising. If you're already practising it, take time to understand the best way to pass it across.

Be a Bible Christian and not a system Christian

50 People Every Christian Should Know, p. 49
CHARLES SIMEON
IN WARREN W. WIERSBE

Spoiler alert! Several denominational doctrines are unbiblical at best or antibiblical at worst. Remember that the Bible is still the Christian's constitution.

We never reach the innermost room in any man's soul
by the expediencies of the showman or the buffoon
The way of irreverence will never lead to the Holy Place

50 People Every Christian Should Know, p. 285
JOHN HENRY JOWETT
IN WARREN W. WIERSBE

Music and comedy have their proper place and mustn't replace God's Word, which is the vehicle of Salvation. Also, they shouldn't be allowed to turn the House of God into an amusement park or dance club.

You have been asked to take notice of the sayings of dying men
— this is mine:
that a life spent in the Service of God and communion with Him
is the most pleasant life that anyone can live in this world

50 People Every Christian Should Know, p. 29
MATTHEW HENRY
IN WARREN W. WIERSBE

This is a testimony of wisdom to young and old.

A good book is like a seed: it produces fruit that has in it seed for more fruit
It is not a picture on the wall
it is a window that invites us to wider horizons

50 People Every Christian Should Know, p. 322
OSWALD CHAMBERS
IN WARREN W. WIERSBE

All books aren't good. First, discover the good ones. Next, start reading. Today is the best day to design a suitable reading plan.

I am realizing more and more
the futility of separating a life into secular and sacred. It is all His

50 People Every Christian Should Know, p. 323
OSWALD CHAMBERS
IN WARREN W. WIERSBE

This dichotomy looks like an unintended consequence of man's limited knowledge. We must endeavour to live consistently in both "secular" or "sacred" avenues.

Never make a principle out of your own experience
let God be as original with other people as He is with you

---

50 People Every Christian Should Know, p. 326
OSWALD CHAMBERS
IN WARREN W. WIERSBE

This is a mistake even the best of men can run into. One preventive measure is sticking close to the principles revealed in the Bible. Allow others to seek and know God for themselves. Don't be an obstacle: intentionally or unintentionally. Examine yourself today.

How much richer we would be
if we would refuse the books of the hour
and discover again the books of the ages

---

50 People Every Christian Should Know, p. 84
WARREN W. WIERSBE

As Richard Wurmbrand succinctly puts it, "Christian books are like good wine, the older the better." A book of the hour which isn't shallow is a true rarity.

The applause of the crowd is not always the approval of the Lord

---

50 People Every Christian Should Know, p. 370
WARREN W. WIERSBE

Never get carried away by the appreciation and praise of the majority. God isn't primarily out to reward motivational speakers.

Watchman Nee

...with God the end never justifies the means

The Normal Christian Life, p. 119
WATCHMAN NEE

A deed is done in God's Name doesn't automatically have His approval; regardless of the doer's sincerity and selflessness. We need to carefully watch our actions.

...the Gospel of grace and the Gospel of the kingdom
must be joined together
In the Gospels, these two were never separated
Only in later years does it seem as if
those who have heard the Gospel of grace
know little or nothing of the Gospel of the kingdom

The Release of The Spirit, p. 62-63
WATCHMAN NEE

We mustn't pick and choose portions of Scriptures to suit our whims and fancies. There has to be a balanced perspective.

Increase in eloquence, Bible knowledge and spiritual gift
is not reckoned as increase of Spiritual life

The Spiritual Man
WATCHMAN NEE

Increase of spiritual life is often evidenced by increase in graces more than gifts; an increase in godlikeness more than skilfulness.

In both his walk and work
Heavenly attraction should always be greater than earthly gravitation

The Spiritual Man
WATCHMAN NEE

We must never allow ourselves to be bogged down by the legitimate cares of this life. Our priorities should be sorted in a heavenward direction.

Emotions change as feeling changes, and how rapidly the latter can change
He therefore who lives by emotion lives without principle

The Spiritual Man
WATCHMAN NEE

Those who believe that truth is relative and subjective ought ot reconsider. If truth can be nothing but absolute, else it becomes fancy. Truth is the bedrock of timeless principles.

A Christian needs to remember that in spiritual affairs
nothing is too small to hinder his progress

The Spiritual Man
WATCHMAN NEE

Never take your heavenward journey easy on this side of eternity.

Overstepping the bounds of the Word of God ushers in countless perils!

The Spiritual Man
WATCHMAN NEE

The revealed Scriptures are finite for several reasons: one being to make man humbly dependent on God.

The worst fallacy one can ever commit is to reckon oneself infallible

The Spiritual Man
WATCHMAN NEE

The subject of biblical perfection is one place teachers should guard against this. On the other hand, spiritual leaders should carefully watch their lives in light of this.

Our bodily strength
cannot cope with the demands of spiritual life, work and war
Combat with sin, sinners and the evil spirits sap our vitality
Solely natural resources are inadequate to supply out bodily needs
We must depend on the Life of Christ, for this alone can sustain us

The Spiritual Man
WATCHMAN NEE

This is a lesson often learnt the hard way: through failure.

God hides His Life in His Word
Inasmuch as He is Life, so also is His Word
Should we view God's Word as a teaching, creed or moral standard
it shall not prove very effective in us
No, God's Word must be digested and united with us
in the same manner as is food

The Spiritual Man
WATCHMAN NEE

None can sincerely outgrow the revealed Scriptures. With patience and humility, God will keep unfolding deeper dimensions before the eyes of your mind.

Will Durant

A nation is born stoic, and dies epicurean

The Story of Civilization: Part I, Our Oriental Heritage
Chapter IX, p. 259
WILL DURANT

This has far reaching implications. Concerted pursuit of sensual pleasure as the highest good is one sure way to frustration and destruction.

...philosophy — the attempt of man
to capture something of that total perspective
which in his modest intervals he knows that only Infinity can possess
the brave and hopeless inquiry into the first causes of things
and their final significance ...

The Story of Civilization: Part I, Our Oriental Heritage
Envoi, p. 936
WILL DURANT

Quite an honest and humble way to define philosophy.

Civilizations come and go; they conquer the earth and crumble into dust
but faith survives every desolation

The Story of Civilization: Part II, The Life of Greece
Chapter II, p. 32-33
WILL DURANT

This points to that "something" in man which longs for connection to Someone larger than himself. Empirical evidence suggests that religion is after all not a pursuit of fools and for fools.

As social organization advances
paternal authority and family unity decrease
freedom and individualism grow

The Story of Civilization: Part II, The Life of Greece
Chapter III, p. 50
Will Durant

History has an interesting way of repeating itself: with variations of course. Hegel said that, "What history teaches us is that men have never learned anything from it." Learning from the experience of others isn't necessarily easy. "Experience is the best teacher;" but what a harsh teacher it is. Christians should be wary when integrating societal advances into their lifestyles. The Bible is still there as a filter.

. . . it is hard for beauty to be virtuous

The Story of Civilization: Part II, The Life of Greece
Chapter VIII, p. 184
Will Durant

Beauty is one of God's gifts. It isn't a sin or vice in itself. It can still be virtuous. However, beauty has a subtle way of opening the back door to pride.

As the mad pursuit of wealth destroys the oligarchy
so the excesses of liberty destroy democracy

The Story of Civilization: Part II, The Life of Greece
Chapter XXI, p. 520
Will Durant

What a word of caution to those who see democracy as the ultimate solution to man's problems. There ought to be a balanced consideration its advantages and disadvantages.

When liberty becomes license, dictatorship is near

The Story of Civilization: Part II, The Life of Greece
Chapter XXI, p. 520
Will Durant

Freedom has boundaries on this side of eternity. Anyone who says otherwise is malicious, naive or ignorant.

A long life is not always a blessing...

The Story of Civilization: Part II, The Life of Greece
Chapter XXI, p. 523
WILL DURANT

There are good things which many wish for but don't properly consider the side effects upfront. You might live long to see disaster befall you or (and) your loved ones: even though you might not have been the cause. Also, you might make a big blunder that stains your good record. Vance Havner often talked about "getting home before dark..."

Energy is only half of genius; the other half is harness ...

The Story of Civilization: Part II, The Life of Greece
Chapter XXII, p. 552
WILL DURANT

John Maxwell said, "Talent is never enough." It's only productive when mixed with diligence, dedication, perseverance and the likes.

Greece had ceased to be Greece before it was conquered by Rome

The Story of Civilization: Part II, The Life of Greece
Chapter XXIX, p. 658
WILL DURANT

...the essential cause of the Roman conquest of Greece
was the disintegration of Greek civilization from within
No great nation is ever conquered until it has destroyed itself

The Story of Civilization: Part II, The Life of Greece
Chapter XXIX, p. 659
WILL DURANT

These are succinct ways to pass this message. Couldn't it be that the current mudslinging of "English" civilization and its foundational Judeo-Christian values is our own way of destroying ourselves from within?

Rome remained great
as long as she had enemies who forced her to unity, vision, and heroism
When she had overcome them all
she flourished for a moment and then began to die

The Story of Civilization: Part III, Caesar and Christ
Chapter II, p. 35
Will Durant

Adversity has its blessings after all. Make the best of every situation. Don't whine without learning from it or fold your hands while doing nothing about it.

The increase of wealth conspired with the corruption of politics
to loosen morals and the marriage bond...
Adultery was so common as to attract little attention
unless played up for political purposes
and practically every well-to-do woman had at least one divorce...
Children were now luxuries which only the poor could afford...
Marriage cum manu disappeared
and women divorced their husbands as readily as men their wives

The Story of Civilization: Part III, Caesar and Christ
Chapter VII, p. 134
Will Durant

Rome was full of...women dizzy with freedom
multiplying divorces, abortions, and adulteries
Childlessness was spreading as the ideal of a declining vitality...

The Story of Civilization: Part III, Caesar and Christ
Chapter XI, p. 211
Will Durant

Isn't this eerily similar to today's society? Wealth isn't evil but it has a way of corrupting us at several levels. Women ought to be free to choose. However, misused freedom has grave consequences.

Moral reform is the most difficult and delicate branch of statesmanship
few rulers have dared to attempt it
most rulers have left it to hypocrites and saints

The Story of Civilization: Part III, Caesar and Christ
Chapter XI, p. 221
Will Durant

Leonard Ravenhill said that, "We have politicians, but no statesman..."
Little wonder why most world leaders, at best de-prioritize moral issues,
and at worst deny the existence of morality.

When great men stoop to sentiment the world grows fonder of them
but when sentiment governs policy empires totter

The Story of Civilization: Part III, Caesar and Christ
Chapter XIII, p. 259
WILL DURANT

One natural follow-up question is: what's the probability that the
world will be fond of a leader who sticks to virtuous principles? The
answer is often less than ten percent. Little wonder why most politicians
terribly falter in their moral stance for the sake of votes.

Sanity, like government, needs checks and balances
no mortal can be omnipotent and sane

The Story of Civilization: Part III, Caesar and Christ
Chapter XIII, p. 266
WILL DURANT

As they say, "power corrupts." It has a way of bringing out the vices
a man never knew he had. Is it any wonder that totalitarian regimes
produce more dead citizens, irrespective of the lofty ideals in their propaganda? Alexis de Tocqueville succinctly puts it like this, "...only God can
be omnipotent without danger because his wisdom and justice are always
equal to his power."

...immorality...
exhausts the body and debases the soul, never satisfying either
avarice and luxury have destroyed peace and health
and power has made man only an abler brute

The Story of Civilization: Part III, Caesar and Christ
Chapter XIV, p. 305
WILL DURANT

Pleasure is good, but only when it is consistent with virtue...

The Story of Civilization: Part III, Caesar and Christ
Chapter XIV, p. 305
Will Durant

How often do you hear immorality being used today? It has undergone much cosmetic surgery and metamorphosis to the point of non-recognition. It's been called fling, affair, one-night stand, free love and so on. Little wonder we've succeeded in "emancipating" sexual intercourse from its divine confines, by redefining marriage through legislative means. Immorality exhausts the body alright but who's talking about its stain on the soul? When we've convinced ourselves that man is only a physical being with no spiritual dimension, discussions about man's soul have been shipped into oblivion. Few non-religious people today are sincere enough to own immorality's devastating effects on the soul. We've found ways of "widening life without deepening it," hurtling and cheering it on in pursuit of luxurious pleasures.

Read good books many times, rather than many books...

The Story of Civilization: Part III, Caesar and Christ
Chapter XIV, p. 306
Will Durant

One of Francis Bacon's quotes is apt here: "Some books are to be tasted, others to be swallowed, and some few to be chewed and digested." Don't waste your precious time on materials that add nothing to your life.

A good wife is a rare bird...stranger than a white cow

The Story of Civilization: Part III, Caesar and Christ
Chapter XX, p. 438
Will Durant

May God help the sincere, unmarried man find a good wife. Also, may God help the sincere, unmarried woman find a good husband. To the married woman, are you a good wife to your husband?

A great civilization is not conquered from without
until it has destroyed itself within

The Story of Civilization: Part III, Caesar and Christ
Epilogue, p. 665
WILL DURANT

This is still true today. It is a warning to those tinkering with society's fabric in the name of progress, oblivious of the strands that are falling off.

...distance...lends enchantment to the view...

The Story of Civilization: Part IV, The Age of Faith
Chapter IV, p. 82
WILL DURANT

This complements the quote which says that, "Familiarity breeds contempt." Desire plus distance has a way of beautifying a thing using the brush of imagination. However, this evaporates once familiarity sets in.

Civilization is a union of soil and soul
— the resources of the earth transformed by the desire and discipline of men

---

The Story of Civilization: Part IV, The Age of Faith
Chapter XI, p. 206
WILL DURANT

This is one interesting way to define civilization.

Religion helped law and the family to turn the animal into a citizen

---

The Story of Civilization: Part IV, The Age of Faith
Chapter XX, p. 506
WILL DURANT

Could it be that our irreligiosity today is helping turn the citizen back into an animal? Just a food for thought.

William Booth

The chief danger of the 20th century will be:
Religion without the Holy Ghost
Christianity without Christ
Forgiveness without repentance
Salvation without regeneration
Politics without God
Heaven without hell

WILLIAM BOOTH

This truth is still relevant today. Make sure you don't lose the essence of a thing in the process or under the guise of refining or improving it.

William Gairdner

When one's word is no longer accepted as one's bond
where cleverness is measured by legal tricks and honesty is cheapened
we are on the way down

The Trouble With Canada... Still, Chapter 4, p. 87
WILLIAM GAIRDNER

Breakthroughs in science and technology hasn't, can't, and won't teach us honesty and integrity. Think that one over. May it not be that our societal advancement is hurtling us towards collapse? It looks as if our physical advancement has outpaced our moral stability.

As faith in God and the afterlife weakened
it would be replaced by faith in human beings and their governments

The Trouble With Canada... Still, Chapter 6, p. 144
WILLIAM GAIRDNER

Man is both a spiritual and physical being. Those who deny the spiritual dimension often replace it by an all-encompassing faith in the physical. As Aristotle said, "Nature abhors a vacuum." However, have you noticed how most life-changing transformations are attributable to a non-physical source? Carefully consider this when next someone castigates you for believing that man has a spiritual dimension.

Great nations spring from great principles

The Trouble With Canada... Still, Chapter 16, p. 494
WILLIAM GAIRDNER

Who cares about principles in this day and age of feel-goodism? What principles are you talking about when many hold the doctrine that truth is relative?

> ...science can measure only what is measurable
> and the most important things in human life are not

The War Against The Family, p. xiii
William Gairdner

Science is good in its proper place. However, a hyper-faith in science as the panacea for societal malady might eventually turn out to be cancerous. Can science give you compelling reasons to be truthful and to honour others?

> In the pure financial sense
> the family is the original and still unequalled
> charitable organization of the world
> No State could possibly match its contribution...

The War Against The Family, p. 92
William Gairdner

The family voluntarily takes care of newborn citizens until they can stand on their own. The family helps relatives or acquaintances with a detailed attention no corporate body can economically provide. Little wonder that our society is losing touch with the poor and afflicted after disdaining the family and making laws which discourage people from seeking married and staying married. All these public-relation stunts masqueraded as corporate social responsibility by some multinational companies do little to affect those who really need help. I think it's high time we rethought this whole thing.

> ...those who teach moral relativism to the young
> are creating tomorrow's moral imbeciles
> By the time we find out whether or not this is true, it will be too late

The War Against The Family, p. 239
William Gairdner

Quite a way to put it. The sad part is that those who feed this to the young today might not be around to bear or witness the consequences of their doctrines.

I would hate to be a woman
My wife says she would hate to be a man
I think this has something to do with why we have a good marriage

---

The War Against The Family, p. 295
WILLIAM GAIRDNER

This is the way God intended it. All this cry for gender equality, neutrality and fluidity is an express-way to confuse both sexes and aggravate their age-long war. Little wonder why many marriages are crumbling today.

Propagandists the world over waste little time on the present generation
They go straight for the fresh young minds, hungry for approval
and eager to digest whatever belief system adults wish to feed them

---

The War Against The Family, p. 356
WILLIAM GAIRDNER

This is a forewarning to parents, mentors and teacher of the young. If you don't "woo" your children to righteousness today, plenty "mind-benders" out there will lead them down the road of destruction.

...[the] world...has elevated personal gratification
to a near theological status...

The War Against The Family, p. 369
WILLIAM GAIRDNER

Don't think that you can't fall into this trap as a Christian. Daily examine your life under the Light of Scriptures.

Neutrality, after all
is really just a coward's vote for the confusion of the status quo...

The War Against The Family, p. 416
WILLIAM GAIRDNER

Neutrality isn't always a viable option in life. Now is the time to get personal convictions that are informed by Scriptures.

Unguided by any standard of virtue outside ourselves
we soon end up with a mere love of our own appetites

The War Against The Family, p. 532
William Gairdner

...human history is a sad lesson
in how moral standards fail in the absence of moral absolutes

The War Against The Family, p. 597
William Gairdner

Little wonder how dark atrocities increase as those who believe we live in a post-truth culture of no absolutes increase. Suicide is now legalized such that a patient can boldly request its administration. All manner of sexual intercourse is glorified over our airwaves. Aren't we already experiencing failing moral standards?

William Gurnall

It requires more prowess and greatness of spirit to obey God faithfully
than to command an army of men
to be a Christian, than to be a captain

The Christian In Complete Armour, p. 3
WILLIAM GURNALL

Many think that Christianity is for losers, weaklings and dullards. How can someone who daily dies to himself be a weakling? Isn't this the dream of philosophers down through the ages? You know, many of these accusers will turn out as hypocrites when placed, even on the balance of reason.

The Christian must not be of such a complying nature
to cut the coat of his profession according to the fashion of the times
or the humour of the company he falls into...

The Christian In Complete Armour, p. 4
WILLIAM GURNALL

The tenets of Christianity are called truths for a reason. They are time-tested and absolute. You're already in a quandary if you claim to be a Christian and want to be everyone's favourite. Would you remain a Christian at the risk of offending others or please them at the expense of your Christianity? Nevertheless, you can't sit on the fence or have it both ways.

God may deny further degrees of strength
to put thee on the exercise of that thou hast more carefully

The Christian In Complete Armour, p. 23
WILLIAM GURNALL

Have you been properly utilizing your God-given gifts? Are you letting them lie fallow? Examine yourself today.

... conversation begets affection
some by this have been brought to marry those
whom at first they thought they could not have liked

The Christian In Complete Armour, p. 48
WILLIAM GURNALL

This is a warning to unmarried folks who are seeking marriage. Be wary and deliberate in choosing your close associates. They will affect your destiny: for good or bad. Quick question: who are your intimates?

No greater plague can befall a man than power without grace

The Christian In Complete Armour, p. 100
WILLIAM GURNALL

The Bible gives several examples. Let's consider Samson and Saul. Samson was divinely gifted with superhuman strength. Saul was gifted with Israel's throne. Both knew the bounds within which God circumscribed their gifts. However, they neglected their need for grace and made shipwreck of their missions. What a sad end they both met!

... every private family is as a little nursery to the church
if the nursery be not carefully planted, the orchard will soon decay

The Christian In Complete Armour, p. 115
WILLIAM GURNALL

This is a plain truth that's often neglected. Parents, God gave you those children for a reason. Please don't shirk or pass off your responsibility to the Sunday school, daycare or someone else. You will be held accountable. Don't allow Church activities and meetings to swallow the time meant for family devotion and discipleship.

The gate into Christ's school is low...

The Christian In Complete Armour, p. 120
WILLIAM GURNALL

Notice that it doesn't say fence, but gate. Many would have easily jumped over the fence. However, you need to bend low in humility to pass through the gate. This often comes with much wiggling and wriggling in discomfort and determination.

... he is the best student in divinity, that studies most upon his knees

The Christian In Complete Armour, p. 121
WILLIAM GURNALL

This ensures the student remains humble and reliant on God. Also, it makes him the first partaker of the lesson he plans on teaching others.

Since man was turned out of paradise
he can do nothing without labour, except sin

The Christian In Complete Armour, p. 121
WILLIAM GURNALL

What an interesting observation. Little wonder it's an uphill battle to do good.

Godliness is the child of truth
and it must be nursed, if we will have it thrive
with no other milk than that of its own mother

The Christian In Complete Armour, p. 133
WILLIAM GURNALL

A man, church, family or nation will not rise higher in godliness than its openness to truth. Notice the use of the metaphor, "child." None ever exhausts the curricula of the school of godliness before leaving earth. There are ever increasing grades. You don't have to abandon your studies or become a truant at the playground of sin because some people drop out.

Satan commonly stops the ear from hearing sound doctrine
before he opens it to embrace corrupt

The Christian In Complete Armour, p. 135
WILLIAM GURNALL

As someone said, "There are no perfect churches. If someone shows you a perfect church, don't go there; because you will make it imperfect..." Don't allow those prickly issues in your local congregation make you relocate to a gathering where error is the rule.

[Pride]...can take sanctuary in the holiest actions
and hide itself under the skirt of virtue itself

The Christian In Complete Armour, p. 136
William Gurnall

This is a call for careful examination of our motives. Hypocrisy can don a garb so holy as to fool even the wearer.

A gracious heart pursues earthly things with a holy indifference
saving the violence and zeal of his spirit for the things of heaven...

The Christian In Complete Armour, p. 157
William Gurnall

This is no excuse for a Christian to become useless and unproductive on earth: far from it. The key point is conserving your energy for the right priorities.

The preacher must read and study his people
as diligently as any book in his study...

The Christian In Complete Armour, p. 164
William Gurnall

Isn't this one reason why some can't connect with their congregation? Their messages have little relevance to the people's circumstances. Similarly, how would a preacher pray aright without knowing what to pray for?

Sacrifice without obedience is sacrilege

The Christian In Complete Armour, p. 183
William Gurnall

It is sacrilege for several reasons. One of which is that the offerer can cover the stench of his evils with the scent of sacrifices. Therefore, obedience ought to come before sacrifice.

...hypocrisy often takes up her lodging next door to sincerity
and so she passes unfound
the soul not suspecting hell can be so near heaven

The Christian In Complete Armour, p. 247
WILLIAM GURNALL

...hypocrisy is a weed with which the best soil is so tainted
that it needs daily care and dressing to keep it under

The Christian In Complete Armour, p. 272
WILLIAM GURNALL

This ought to spur every Christian to daily examine their lives under the Light of Scriptures. George Whitefield said that, "the best of men are but men at the best..."

The moralist is very punctual in his dealings with men
but very thievish in his carriage to God
though he will not wrong his neighbour of a farthing
he sticks not to rob God of greater matters
his love, fear, faith, are due debts to God
but he makes no conscience of paying them

The Christian In Complete Armour, p. 259
WILLIAM GURNALL

A moralist shouldn't be mistaken for a Christian. He appears to get the "horizontal" component right but misses the prerequisite and most important "vertical" component. Isn't this a challenge to Christians whose moral standards are lower than those of these moralists? Jesus Christ emphasises this in Matthew 5:20, "For I say unto you, That except your righteousness shall exceed the righteousness of the scribes and Pharisees, ye shall in no case enter into the kingdom of heaven."

The hypocrite sets his watch, not by the sun, the word, I mean
but by the town-clock; what most do, that he will be easily persuaded to do
vox populi is his vox Dei

The Christian In Complete Armour, p. 278
WILLIAM GURNALL

A Christian's principle and practice ought not to be swayed by the latest fads in society. Rather, the Bible should be his life's umpire.

An idle man does none good, and himself most hurt

The Christian In Complete Armour, p. 312
WILLIAM GURNALL

In extension, much harm will be done to others when he finally acts out the convoluted thoughts which have accumulated over time.

Be humble when thou art most holy...
Never art thou less holy, than when puffed up with the conceit of it

The Christian In Complete Armour, p. 341
WILLIAM GURNALL

C. S. Lewis in "The Screwtape Letters" speaks of a man taking "...pride at his own humility..." Mishandled holiness can breed one of the subtlest kinds of pride.

The highest created throne that God can sit in is the soul of a believer...

The Christian In Complete Armour, p. 350
WILLIAM GURNALL

What an honour and privilege! This is one reason why man isn't a mere animal like the beasts. Is your heart God's throne today? Are you more interested in elevating God everywhere else except where it matters most?

O Christians, agree together, and your number will increase

The Christian In Complete Armour, p. 400
WILLIAM GURNALL

The emphasis on corporate evangelism with oblique references to Christian unity doesn't often go down well in my spirit. If the so-called souls are won, where would they be nurtured? Is it in a congregation riddled with rancour and vainglory? I believe that numeric growth would naturally happen if the right conditions are in place. It's just like seed and soil. No matter how promising that seed is, a harsh soil will stunt its growth; or even worse, kill it.

And no mean price useth to be set on the head of liberty
the very birds had rather be abroad in the woods with liberty
though lean with cold and care, to pick up here and there a little livelihood
than in a golden cage with all their attendance

The Christian In Complete Armour, p. 407
WILLIAM GURNALL

As Vance Havner once said, "The Fathers of 1776 risked security to win liberty, but we are selling liberty to win security. We would rather be fat birds in a cage than lean birds in the woods. We are trading our birthright for a mess of pottage, piling up possessions without and becoming paupers within."

No such picklock to open the heart as love

The Christian In Complete Armour, p. 421
WILLIAM GURNALL

Love prevails where and when force fails. Force tries gaining entrance by breaking the door or lock. It only succeeds to meet an room empty. However, it often fails to break either lock or door. Conversely, love picks the lock and finds a well-prepared room awaiting its entrance.

Faith is not lazy
it inclines not the soul to sleep, but work
it sends the creature not to bed
there to sleep away his time in ease and sloth
but into the field

The Christian In Complete Armour, p. 446
WILLIAM GURNALL

Faith and work aren't mutually exclusive. They are two sides of the same coin.

...temptations are the breathings of the devil's wrath

The Christian In Complete Armour, p. 477
WILLIAM GURNALL

...there is a spark of hell in every temptation

The Christian In Complete Armour, p. 477
WILLIAM GURNALL

These definitions paint a clear picture of temptation's deadliness.

The fowler lays the trap, but the bird's own desire betrays it into the net

---

The Christian In Complete Armour, p. 478
WILLIAM GURNALL

Temptation isn't sin so long as a man doesn't yield to it. Be spiritually sensitive to discern these traps for what they are.

A silly child playing with a lighted straw
may set a house on fire, which many wise men cannot quench
And truly Satan may use thy folly and carelessness
to kindle lust in another's heart
Perhaps an idle, light speech drops from thy mouth
and thou meanest no great hurt
but a gust of temptation may carry this spark into thy friend's bosom
and kindle a sad fire there
A wanton attire, perhaps naked breasts and shoulders
which we will suppose thou wearest with a chaste heart
and only because it is the fashion
yet may ensnare another's eye
And if he that kept a pit open but to the hurt of a beast, sinned
how much more thou, who givest occasion to a soul's sin
which is a worse hurt?

The Christian In Complete Armour, p. 479
WILLIAM GURNALL

This message on godly comportment is self-explanatory and needs no additional commentary. It even addresses the self-deluded "Christian" who places the onus on others to guard their hearts simply to justify his narcissism.

...the lust of the flesh, the lust of the eye, and the pride of life...
called by some the worldling's trinity

The Christian In Complete Armour, p. 479
WILLIAM GURNALL

This is a commentary on 1 John 2:15-17; with respect to what unbelievers yield their lives.

A good man is as good as his word...
he is a just man that keeps his word...

The Christian In Complete Armour, p. 486, 504
WILLIAM GURNALL

This truth has fallen on evil times today, even among Christians.

...when Christ suffered, justice and mercy met...

The Christian In Complete Armour, p. 503
WILLIAM GURNALL

This is one way to explain the mysteries of the incarnation and crucifixion. God as Man, suffered the justice due to man for man's sins, to bring God's redemptive mercy to man.

...how can there be great faith, where there is little faithfulness?

The Christian In Complete Armour, p. 513
WILLIAM GURNALL

Every Christian can do this one: plain old faithfulness.

It is on a watery cloud
that the sun paints those curious colours in the rainbow

The Christian In Complete Armour, p. 524
WILLIAM GURNALL

Adversity could be the right condition in God's Omniscience to beautifully display His Omnipotence in your life.

And I am sure he buys gold too dear
that pays the peace of his conscience for the purchase

The Christian In Complete Armour, p. 526
WILLIAM GURNALL

This points to the boundary a Christian ought not to cross in his pursuit of wealth; or any man for that matter. John Wooden once said that, "There is no pillow as soft as a clear conscience."

For my own part, I think it more wisdom
to borrow a sword of proved metal at another's hands
than to go with a weak leaden one of my own into the field
and come home beaten for my folly and pride

The Christian In Complete Armour, p. 563
WILLIAM GURNALL

True humility will save you from much foolishness.

...the grossest heresies have bred in the finest wits

The Christian In Complete Armour, p. 585
WILLIAM GURNALL

Much learning is no sure shield against error. Man is still fallible on this side of eternity.

God's wounds cure, — sin's kisses kill

The Christian In Complete Armour, p. 590
WILLIAM GURNALL

What an irony! On one hand, God doesn't always wound and His wounds aren't always deadly. On the other hand, sin always kills and uses kisses as temporary anaesthetics while inflicting deadly wounds.

It is one of the devil's best policies
by sinking the price of errors in the thoughts of men
to make them thereby the more vendible

The Christian In Complete Armour, p. 600
WILLIAM GURNALL

Without sacrificing much meaning, price here can be seen as consequence. This policy could be achieved by popularising and glamorising error to the point of familiarity. As Matthew Henry said, "Familiarity, even with that which is most awful, is apt to breed contempt." It dangerously desensitizes men's consciences.

Now, in comparing scripture with scripture
be careful thou interpret obscure places by the more plain and clear
and not the clear by the dark

The Christian In Complete Armour, p. 602
WILLIAM GURNALL

There are many things our limited minds can't fully comprehend in the Scriptures while on earth. However, this is one good principle that will help preserve our faith.

That which may pass for diligence
in a private Christian's search into the Scriptures
may be charged as negligence upon the minister

The Christian In Complete Armour, p. 620
WILLIAM GURNALL

O how shall the people grow, if the minister doth not?
and how shall he grow, if he doth not daily drink in more than he pours out?

The Christian In Complete Armour, p. 621
WILLIAM GURNALL

It is often foolhardy to compare oneself with others. One reason being that the potential God has placed in each person tallies with His expectation from the same.

The Christian's armour will rust
except it be furbished with the oil of prayer

The Christian In Complete Armour, p. 624
WILLIAM GURNALL

This shows how prayer functions as a spiritual polish and lubricant.

Prayer is the saint's exercise-field, where his graces are breathed
it is as the wind to the air, it brightens the soul
as bellows to the fire, which clears the coal of those ashes that smother them

The Christian In Complete Armour, p. 627
WILLIAM GURNALL

This shows how prayer functions as a spiritual purgative.

...God's purpose to give doth not discharge us from our duty to ask...

The Christian In Complete Armour, p. 630
WILLIAM GURNALL

This is consistent with God's grant of freewill to man. Prayer opens a two-way channel between God and man.

Prayer is an humble appeal from our impotency to God's omnipotence

The Christian In Complete Armour, p. 631
WILLIAM GURNALL

There are three key points here: man's humility, man's impotency, God's omnipotence. How can a man acknowledge his impotency without humility? Prayer is an avenue for man to express his impotency to God and tap into God's omnipotence.

Positively, to pray in faith
is to ask of God, in the name of Christ, what he hath promised
relying on his power and truth for performance
without binding him up to time, manner, or means

The Christian In Complete Armour, p. 657
WILLIAM GURNALL

Notice three key points here: timing, manner, and means. This sheds light on the proper understanding of prayer. God isn't at any man's beck and call. His answers might not be according to our whims and fancies; but "blessed is he whosoever shall not be offended in. . . " Him, according to Matthew 11:6 and Luke 7:23.

Man may propose and purpose, but God disposeth

The Christian In Complete Armour, p. 672
WILLIAM GURNALL

Just as the Bible says in Lamentations 3:37, "Who is he that saith, and it cometh to pass, when the Lord commandeth it not?" King Nebuchadnezzar in Daniel 4:1-37 and the rich fool in Luke 12:16-21 learnt this lesson the hard way.

I will not enter into a discourse how often a Christian should pray in a day
at least it must be twice, that is, morning and night
Prayer must be the key of the morning, and lock of the night

The Christian In Complete Armour, p. 673
WILLIAM GURNALL

A variant of this quote is found in Philip Henry's biography which was written by Matthew Henry, his son. It says, "Let prayer be the key of the morning, and the bolt of the night." From these, a case for praying at least twice a day could be made.

His zeal is false, that seems hot against sin, but is cold to holiness

---

The Christian In Complete Armour, p. 725
WILLIAM GURNALL

The demarcation between sin and holiness is a chasm and not a fence. Hence, there is no fence-sitting or having the best of both worlds. Notwithstanding how hypocrisy paints this chasm so thin as to look like a fence.

A still-born child is no heir...

The Christian In Complete Armour, p. 747
WILLIAM GURNALL

All who claim to be the Lord's and do good works in His Name need to properly examine their lives. Were you ever safely birthed by the Holy Spirit or were you still-born or aborted? Only those successfully born by the Holy Spirit would inherit the Kingdom of God.

It were well if this were only the heathen's sin
but by woful experience we find that the true Christian
hath not more cruel enemies in the whole world than some of his own name
The sharpest persecutions of the church
have been by those that were in the church

The Christian In Complete Armour, p. 783
WILLIAM GURNALL

O! Christian, are you an unintentional persecutor of the righteous? Now is the best time to examine your actions and attitudes under the Light of Scriptures.

...charity may begin, though it must not end at home

The Christian In Complete Armour, p. 787
WILLIAM GURNALL

We ought to do good to as many as God brings our way and as much as He has equipped us.

Samson's strength lay not in a single hair, but his whole lock...

The Christian In Complete Armour, p. 789
WILLIAM GURNALL

This is an interesting way to emphasize the importance of unity. It shows how we need the combination of gifts God has uniquely placed in each believer to be truly effective as the Church. Also, it is applicable to the right use of Scriptures.

The sins of teachers are the teachers of sin...

The Christian In Complete Armour, p. 792
Wᴵᴸᴸᴵᴬᴹ Gᵁᴿᴺᴬᴸᴸ

The minister's practice makes a greater sound than his doctrine
They who forget his sermon, will remember his example
to quote it for their apology, when time serves

The Christian In Complete Armour, p. 793
Wᴵᴸᴸᴵᴬᴹ Gᵁᴿᴺᴬᴸᴸ

A timely warning for parents and leaders to carefully watch over their lives. Your practice speaks louder than your preaching or profession, and will serve as precedent for the ignorant, naive and crafty.

To over-do, is the ready way to undo

The Christian In Complete Armour, p. 797
Wᴵᴸᴸᴵᴬᴹ Gᵁᴿᴺᴬᴸᴸ

Zeal that isn't guarded and guided by wisdom and knowledge causes more harm than good. It will eventually mar the picture it spent precious time and resources painting.

Error is but a day younger than truth

The Christian In Complete Armour, p. 797-798
Wᴵᴸᴸᴵᴬᴹ Gᵁᴿᴺᴬᴸᴸ

Wherever you see truth, error isn't far behind. This is one reason to jealously guard the truth you've tried and tested.

The gospel is a mystery, therefore rest not in thy present attainments
either in thy knowledge, as it is a mystery of faith
or thy practice, as it is a mystery of godliness...
The gospel hath respect both to the head and heart, understanding and will
to the understanding, it is a mystery of faith
to the heart and life, it is a mystery of godliness

The Christian In Complete Armour, p. 802, 806
William Gurnall

Notice the fullness and beauty the gospel brings into a life: mental, emotional, spiritual, and so on. Also, it keeps unfolding more bounties to the willing life. Keep hungering and thirsting for more! God has promised fulfilment in Matthew 5:6, "Blessed are they which do hunger and thirst after righteousness: for they shall be filled."

...many speak one word for Christ, and two for themselves

The Christian In Complete Armour, p. 809
William Gurnall

Preacher, are you guilty of this on the pulpit? Christian, are you guilty of this in your daily living and testimony? May we never forget whose ambassadors we are.

We must come to good works by faith
and not to faith by good works

The Christian In Complete Armour, p. 809
William Gurnall

Although faith and good works aren't mutually exclusive, there is a profitable and divinely approved sequence. This is one reason why natural philanthropy, though good, grants the doer no saving faith in this world nor a reward in the world to come.

Indeed, the purity of Christians' lives
is the best attractive to win others to the love of religion
Had Christ's doves more sweet spices
of humility, charity, patience and other heavenly graces in their wings
as they fly about in the world
they would soon bring more company home with them
This is the gold that should over-lay the temple of Christ's church
and would make others in love with its beauty
this was one happy means
for the incredible increase of converts in the primitive times
Then the mystery of the gospel was made known
not only by the apostles' powerful preaching
but by Christians' holy living

The Christian In Complete Armour, p. 810-811
William Gurnall

I say a big Amen! Couldn't this be one key reason we aren't experiencing sustained and genuine numeric growth today in the Church?

William James

The more mind does, the more it can do

WILLIAM JAMES

The mind is like mental muscle. It grows stronger by exercise. A baby can do so little for himself because his muscles haven't done much exercise. Don't allow you physical growth to outpace your mental growth.

Index List

H

Q

R

S